中国国家汉办规划教材
体验汉语系列教材

体验®汉语

Experiencing Chinese

写作教程（初级2）

总策划　刘　援
主　编　陈作宏
编　者　陈作宏　张　璟　邓秀均

高等教育出版社
Higher Education Press

《体验汉语®》立体化系列教材

教材规划委员会

许　琳	曹国兴	刘　辉	刘志鹏
马箭飞	宋永波	邱立国	刘　援

体验汉语写作系列教材

《体验汉语写作教程(初级2)》

主　　编	陈作宏
编　　者	陈作宏　张　璟　邓秀均

总 策 划	刘　援
策划编辑	祝大鸣　梁　宇
责任编辑	梁　宇
封面设计	王凌波
版式设计	刘　艳
插图选配	梁　宇
插图绘画	九月天空
责任校对	梁　宇
责任印制	陈伟光

亲爱的老师：

您好！欢迎您使用《体验汉语写作教程》系列教材。希望您和您的学生在使用本系列教材的过程中有所收获，并得到愉悦的体验。

学习汉语的最佳途径就是以言行事，学习者应当在使用汉语的过程中学会汉语。因此，本系列教材力求体现体验式教学的现代教育理念，为您提供任务型的教学方案。

书面表达是语言学习者不可或缺的一项语言交际技能。随着留学生教育的发展和留学生数量的不断增加，有写作需求的学习者越来越多。在听、说、读、写四种语言技能中，人们往往对写的技能重视不够。写作课通常只在高年级开设，使得学习者的书面表达能力严重滞后，从而影响了他们汉语交际能力的继续提高。而汉语书面表达能力的提高，对学习者整体语言交际能力的提高能够起到积极的促进作用，也能使口语水平上一个更高的层次，表达更准确、更规范。因此，为了跟上对外汉语教学发展的步伐，满足学习者的需求，《体验汉语写作教程》力求分阶段、有计划地提高学习者的书面表达能力，巩固他们在其他语言技能课上所学的知识，以促进学习者汉语交际能力的全面发展。

本系列教材共六册，分初、中、高三级，每级分上下两册。本教材采取循环递进的方式，提高学生在书面表达方面的叙述、说明和议论的能力。初级阶段旨在帮助学生把学到的汉字、语法、词汇方面的汉语知识导入到书面表达中；中级阶段的目标是丰富学生各种语段类型的写作经验，同时训练学生汉语表达的准确性；高级阶段从一般的语段、语篇训练向真正意义上的记叙文、说明文、议论文的写作过渡，并有效提高表达的得体性。

为方便您使用，《体验汉语写作教程》每册编写了15课，还为您提供了可以灵活选用的复习课，以及足够数量的课外作业。本系列教材可以与综合课和其他技能课配合使用，也可以用于选修课教学。使用对象为外国留学生中的长期进修生。

为了您能更好地使用本系列教材，下面介绍一下本教材的特点以及一些使用方面的建议。

教材特点

1. 依据《高等学校外国留学生汉语教学大纲·长期进修》中的词汇、语法和功能项目确定教学等级、教材内容和难度，因而可以配合多种教材使用。

2. 以实用的书面表达任务为编写主线，并将语言运用与语篇形式及表达功能等项目综合起来确定教学内容。

3. 采用以任务为中心的体验式课堂教学模式，设计了以意义为中心的、贴近真实生活的任务活动，以提升课堂教学的互动性和交际性。

4. 选取贴近留学生生活和中国国情、文化等留学生关注的话题，语言材料丰富生动。

5. 采用丰富的书面表达训练方式，循序渐进地给学习者提供书面表达的机会，并提供各种辅助手段帮助他们顺利完成任务，逐渐消除学生的畏难情绪。

6. 为了使学生可以在教学过程中充分体验到写作的乐趣，本系列教材关注人们在写作过程中所经过的不同阶段，每一课的课堂活动都是按照启发、引导和体会写作过程的思路设计的。

7. 为了节省教师备课的时间，每一课的教学内容和活动都与实际的课堂教学步骤同步，并提供了教学时间和教学安排方面的相关提示供教师参考。

本教材在编写过程中，本着吸收以往写作教材的优点、克服弊端的宗旨，从方便教师使用，促使学生爱用的角度，对教学内容和教学环节用心地作了细致的处理，希望能取得更好的效果。

使用建议

1. 建议您每一课用两课时完成，每五课进行一次总结和讲评。每次课前可用5分钟左右简短讲评上一课作业中的主要问题。建议每册授课课时为36到40课时，每周完成一课的教学内容。您可以从零起点班级开始，每周两课时，每学期使用一册；也可以每周4课时，每学期集中使用同一等级的两册教材。

2. 教材各环节中标示的时间仅供您参考。您可以根据课堂情况进行调整。如果您觉得时间不够用，可让学生课前预习词语和语言形式部分。

3. 语言形式不是教学重点，但可以帮助学生就某一话题更好地进行表达。您可以根据学生的语言程度有重点地处理这一部分的活动。

4. 教材中"给老师的提示"仅供您在教学过程中参考，也许您会有更好的处理方式。

5. 教材中的"提示"可能需要您给学生适当讲解一下，提醒他们注意。

6. 作业环节您可以根据时间灵活处理，留给学生课外完成或者在课堂上做一定的准备。

7. 复习课您可以与总结讲评一起进行，那样会产生更好的效果。

8. 因为教学时间安排较紧，因此，您批改学生作业时所给的评语和建议非常重要。

希望您能喜欢这套教材，也希望您将使用过程中发现的问题告诉我们。欢迎您随时和我们联系，并提出您的批评和建议。

编　者

2006年10月

Dear students,

We are very glad that you are using *Experiencing Chinese Writing Course*. No matter whether you love or hate writing, we sincerely hope that you will make significant progress in your Chinese writing and enjoy your writing experience using this textbook.

Perhaps you think speaking is more important than writing. However, if you do not learn how to write, it will be hard to improve your Chinese beyond a certain degree. That is to say, learning writing plays a positive role in improving Chinese communicative skills and is even helpful for improving your oral communication.

We believe that the best way to study Chinese is learning by doing — learning by using the language. For this purpose, we have prepared a number of meaningful activities for you and your classmates to complete using Chinese. During this course you will experience the pleasure of using Chinese, and at the same time improve your Chinese writing skills. In each lesson we have included several sections. Each section is like a step. After finishing each lesson, you will have stepped up to a new level, and you will experience success and enjoyment in the course of continuous improvements.

Experiencing Chinese Writing Course is different from other textbooks. It requires your active participation in activities, not passive reading and listening. You will become more and more confident through these activities, because you will find your writing skills to be far better than you thought.

In using the textbook, you should pay attention to the following:

1. Get along with your classmates.

2. When you have questions or ideas in class, speak out bravely and discuss with your classmates.

3. Do not be afraid of writing Chinese characters. You can write *Pinyin* first instead of characters, and then look the words up in a dictionary or ask your teacher and classmates.

4. You will complete writing tasks and revise paragraphs together with your classmates. Thus, do not be afraid of letting others see your paragraph. You can learn from and help each other.

5. Practice writing in every lesson and do not give up halfway. You will find your Chinese writing has made great progress after a period of time.

We sincerely hope that you will enjoy writing in Chinese.

Authors
October 2006

《体验汉语写作教程(初级2)》编写说明

教学目标

初级阶段的基本目标是帮助学习者把刚刚学到的汉字、语法、词汇方面的汉语知识导入书面表达中，并有计划地进行书面表达训练，从而为进一步提高学习者的叙述能力、说明能力和议论能力打好基础。

教学对象

初级2册对应于《高等学校外国留学生汉语教学大纲——长期进修》的初等3、4级。适用于经过半年左右汉语学习的外国留学生。

教学内容

以写句子、语段和简单的应用文为主要教学内容。

教材体例

本册由15个正课和3个复习课组成。为方便学习者复习和查阅，书后附有"词汇表"和"汉语常用标点符号一览表"。

一、每课的构成

15个正课均由"学习目标"、"写前准备"、"写作任务"、"讨论修改"和"作业"几个板块组成。

1. **学习目标**：即本课所应该完成的书面表达任务。目的在于帮助学习者明确学习目标。

2. **写前准备**：包括"热身活动"和"语言形式"两个部分。"热身活动"部分的目的在于激活学习者的相关知识，同时帮助他们熟悉主题、预测内容、激发其学习欲望。同时复习和学习完成本课学习目标所需要的词汇。"语言形式"部分直接服务于本课的学习目标，可以帮助学生更好地表达。

3. **写作任务**：包括"组织材料"和"动手写"两个部分。"组织材料"部分通过个人活动和小组活动相结合的方式，帮助学习者整理好在前一个环节中所获得的语言材料，并通过阅读和模仿，将其与自己的实际生活结合起来，形成一个基本完整的想法，以便在"动手写"环节能够在规定的时间里顺利地完成语段。"动手写"环节，将自己在"组织材料"环节所形成的想法写成一篇小短文。

4. 讨论修改：这一部分让学习者在互动的过程中达到互相启发、互相学习的目的，为进一步自主修改和加工短文做好准备。

5. 作业：包括"复习整理"和"补充提高"两个部分。这一部分主要是为了督促学习者在课下复习、总结本课所学的内容。

二、复习课的构成

复习课由"单元自测"、"复习与扩展"和"写作工作室"3个板块组成。

1. 单元自测：这一部分的自测题是为了帮助学习者总结和复习学过的内容，使学习者更有信心地投入下一步的学习。

2. 复习与扩展：这一部分复习所学内容中的重要内容，并在此基础上进行适当的扩展。

3. 写作工作室：这一部分精心设计了一些具有挑战性的写作任务，让学习者有机会体验一下实战写作。

编　者

2006年10月

Introduction

Objectives

The basic objective at the beginning level is to help learners transfer learned Chinese characters, grammar, and vocabulary into writing, and gradually train them in expressive writing, in order to improve narrative and explanative skills and lay a firm foundation for argumentative skills.

Target Learners

Beginning 2 is suitable for Chinese language learners who have studied Chinese for half a year.

Contents

Writing Chinese sentences, paragraphs and simple practical writing are main elements.

Organization

This textbook consists of 15 lessons and 3 review lessons. For the convenience of the learner, a *Punctuation Index* and *Vocabulary Index* are included at the end of the textbook.

Structure of Each Main Lesson:

Each lesson consists of "Objective", "Before Writing", "Writing Task", "After Writing" and "Assignment" sections. We will introduce each section as follows.

1. Objective: Writing tasks are listed here in order to help you clarify the goals.

2. Before Writing: This section consists of two parts: "Warm-Up" and "Language Focus". The "Warm-Up" section aims to activate your related knowledge, familiarize the topic, predict the content, arouse your desire to learn, and at the same time prepare the vocabulary for the lesson's tasks. The "Language Focus" section also serves the objective of the lesson and helps you to express yourself clearly.

3. Writing Task: This section consists of two parts: "Organizing Materials" and "Getting It Down". The "Organizing Materials" section helps you form basic but complete ideas by organizing the language materials obtained from the previous sections and relating them to actual life through individual activities and group activities. In "Getting It Down", you will organize the ideas written in the "Organizing Materials" section to make a short paragraph similar to the example.

4. After Writing: This section aims to elicit interaction and mutual learn, and make preparations for the next step of revising and editing.

5. Assignment: This section consists of two parts: "Review" and "Growing and Improving". This section aims to urge you to review and conclude this lesson after class.

Structure of Review Lesson

Each Review Lesson consists of three sections: "Self-Test", "Review and Extension", "Writing Workshop".

1. Self-Test: This section aims to help you summarize and review what you have learned, and build confidence to learn further.

2. Review and Extension: In this section you will review key points and, based on them, extend your knowledge.

3. Writing Workshop: In this section we have designed some more challenging tasks to give you an opportunity to experience "true" writing.

Authors
October 2006

目 录

学习目标

1

留言条

学习目标 Objective

学习写留言条

Learn to write a note

写前准备 Before Writing

一、热身活动 Warm-Up (约30分钟)

1. 请仔细看看下面的图片，把你想到的重要词语写在对应的图片旁边。
   Look at the following pictures carefully and write the words that come to you next to the pictures.

2. 两人一组，和同伴比较一下，看看你和同伴写的词语一样不一样，然后一起说说图片的内容。
   Work in pairs. Look at whether the words you wrote are the same as your partner's, and then talk about the pictures together.

   ◎ 同伴说的时候，你应该注意听。如果有不知道的词语，一定要问问他(她)。
   Listen to your partner carefully and ask him/her about the words that you don't understand.

3. 根据图片内容，写出下列问题的答案。
Write down the answers to the following questions according to the pictures.

(1) 安娜为什么来找大卫？

_____

(2) 大卫在宿舍吗？

_____

(3) 大卫的同屋可以转告(zhuǎngào to pass on)大卫吗？

_____

(4) 大卫的同屋要出去，安娜怎么办？

_____

❋ 你应该写完整的句子，并尽量用上你
写在图片旁边的词语。
*Write complete sentences and try to use
the words next to the pictures.*

❋ 不会写的字，可以先用拼音写。
*If there are any characters that you
cannot write, you may write them in
Pinyin first.*

4. 和同伴交换课本，互相学习，互相检查。
Exchange textbooks with your partner. Learn and check what he/she has written.

(1) 修改自己写得不好的句子。
Revise your sentences.

(2) 帮助同伴改正错别字，并用汉字替换拼音。
Help your partner correct wrong characters and replace *Pinyin* with characters.

5. 请你试着替安娜写出这个留言条。
   Please write the note for Anne.

● 给老师的提示：您可以请几个学生读一读他们写的留言条，并将教学引入下一个环节，使学生注意如何使用留言条，以及留言条的格式。

二、语言形式 Language Focus （约20分钟）

1. 两人一组，和同伴一起阅读下面的留言条，并说说人们什么时候需要写留言条。
   Work in pairs. Read the following note together and discuss when people might need to write notes.

● 给老师的提示：您可以尽量启发学生说说他们在生活中遇到过的需要写留言条的情况。

留言条

　　有事需要告诉别人，而对方又不在的时候，可以写一张便条加以说明，这就是留言条。一般的留言条是我们在日常生活中，给同事、同学、朋友、邻居、家人等写的，只需要简要说明事情。

Note

A note is written to inform somebody of something when he/she is absent. Common notes are written to co-workers, classmates, friends, neighbors, family members, etc. to explain something in our daily lives.

安妮：

　　今天下午，你北京大学的朋友乔丹给你来过电话，他明天要回国了，问你有没有事儿。他让你晚上给他打电话，电话号码是32016588。

白姗

2006年8月2日

◎ 要注意留言条的格式：
Pay attention to the form of a note:

1. 称呼，一定要顶格写，后面加上冒号。
A greeting should be written at the beginning of the first line and followed by a colon.

2. 另起一行，空两个格，写正文。
Indent the next line of a note two character spaces, and begin to write the text.

3. 在正文的右下方写上留言人的姓名。
A closing should be written on the bottom-right side of the note.

4. 在留言人姓名的下面写上日期。
The date should be written just below the closing.

● 给老师的提示：这一部分您可以带着全班一起完成。并请您参考书后面的"汉语常用标点符号一览表"提醒学生复习一下逗号和句号的用法。

2. 看看你刚才在第4页上写的留言条，并按照正确的格式重新写一遍。
   Look at the note you wrote on page 4 and rewrite it in the correct form.

●给老师的提示：
这一题您可以采取
先写后说的方式进
行，并指导学生表
达得更准确。

写作任务 Writing Task

一、组织材料 Organizing Materials (约20分钟)

1. 假设你原来跟妈妈说好了在家里吃饭，可是现在又不能在家里吃了，请
   写出原因。
   Suppose that you planned to have dinner with your mother at home,
   but now you cannot make it. Write your reasons.

●给老师的提示：
这两题您可以让学
生先说一说，然后
再写。

2. 仔细看看下面的图片，请写出图片中事情的经过。
   Look at the following pictures carefully and write about what happens in the pictures.

   _____

   _____

   _____

   _____

3. 与一个同伴交换课本，看看他(她)是怎么写的。
   Exchange textbooks with your partner to see what he/she has written.

●给老师的提示：学生完成后，您也可以让全班交流一下。

二、动手写 Getting It Down (约20分钟)

1. 仔细看看下面两张留言条，然后大家一起总结一下它们的区别。
   Look at the following two notes and work together to summerize their differences.

王老师：

　　今天上课的时候，我没有写完作业，所以我的本子没有交。现在我已经写完了。下一次我一定按时(ānshí on time)交作业，请老师原谅我。

山本一郎
6月8日下午3点

王明明：

　　听说明天你要去日本出差。下个星期我就要去上海了，如果你今天有时间，咱们下午一起吃饭，好吗？

　　另，如果你的行李(xíngli luggage)比较多，明天我可以去机场送你。

　　回来后，给我打电话吧。我的手机(shǒujī cell phone)一直开着。

李江
3月8日中午1点30分

●给老师的提示：这一题您可以带着大家一起做，并指导学生注意留言条在格式和语言表达上的特点。

2. 模仿上面的留言条，利用你刚才准备的材料，写出下面两张留言条。
   Organize the materials you prepared and write the following two notes, as in the example.

(1) 给妈妈的留言条

(2) 大卫给同屋的留言条

留言条1：

留言条2：

Discussion and Revision （约10分钟）

1. 与同伴交换所写的留言条，看后回答问题。
   Exchange notes with your partner, and then answer the following questions.

   (1) 他(她)写的句子你都能看懂吗？把看不懂的句子画出来，告诉他(她)。

Do you understand everything your partner wrote? Mark the unclear sentences and ask him/her.

(2) 比较一下你们写的留言条，看看你们写的一样不一样。
Compare the notes you wrote with your partner's and see whether they are the same or not.

(3) 你的同伴写的留言条格式正确吗？如果有问题请你告诉他(她)。
Check whether your partner used the correct form. If there are any mistakes, tell him/her.

(4) 你的同伴有没有写错字？有的话就告诉他(她)。
Are there any wrong characters? If there are, tell him/her.

(5) 如果有你不知道的词和不认识的字，就问问他(她)。
If there are any characters you do not recognize, ask him/her.

(6) 看看留言条中的"，"是不是写成"、"或者"."了。
Check whether "，" is written as "、" or "." in his/her notes.

※ 互相检查，改正错误，遇到困难可以问老师。
Check what your partner wrote and correct the errors. Ask your teacher when you encounter difficulties.

2. 改正自己留言条中的错误，然后和其他小组交流一下。
Correct the errors in your notes and then discuss with other groups.

●给老师的提示：您可以请几个学生读一读他们写的留言条，使同学们分享彼此的写作成果。您还可以从学生的文章中总结一些实用的结构写在黑板上，最后做些简单、必要的讲解，作为本课的总结。

作业 Assignment

一、复习整理 Review

1. 整理本课所写过的句子和短文，把错句、错字改正后写在下边。
   Review the sentences and paragraphs you wrote in this lesson, and correct the sentences and characters which were written incorrectly.

2. 整理本课所写过的句子和短文，将生词和新的结构找出来，写在下边，还可以用它们写几个新的句子，帮助自己记忆。
   Review the sentences and paragraphs you wrote in this lesson. Pick out the new words and structures and write them down. Make some new sentences with them to help you memorize them.

二、补充提高 Growing and Improving

1. 对你写的那两个留言条再进行一次补充和修改，然后抄写在作业本上交给老师批改。
   Revise the two notes again and add the new content. Rewrite your notes and hand them in to your teacher.

2. 如果你的生活中有什么事情需要写留言条，别忘了试一试。
   If you encounter some situations in your daily life in which you need to write notes, don't hesitate to have a try.

> 要注意充分利用这一课所学的新词、新结构等，并尽量吸取其他同学文章中的成功之处。
> *Make use of the new words, structures, etc. in this lesson, and try your best to absorb the strong points from what your classmates wrote.*

2

我和我的同屋

学习目标 Objective

学习简单介绍一个人的特点

Learn to introduce a person's characteristics

写前准备 Before Writing

一、热身活动 Warm-Up (约30分钟)

1. 你能从下面的几个方面介绍自己吗？请你简单填写下面的表格，把重要的词语写出来。
   Can you introduce yourself using the following aspects? Fill in the table below with key words.

基本情况 Basic Information	姓名：	年龄：
	性别：	国籍：
兴趣爱好 Interests and Hobbies		
饮食习惯 Eating Habits		
外语学习的经历 Foreign Language Study		
其他 Others		

◎ 写词语，不要写句子。不会写的字，可以先用拼音写。

Write key words instead of sentences. If there are any characters you cannot write, write them in Pinyin first.

2. 两人一组，给同伴介绍一下你自己。
   Work in pairs and introduce yourself to your partner.

3. 仔细看看下面的图片，然后从小词库里选择词语写在合适的图片下边。
Look at the following pictures, and then write the words from the Word Box under the appropriate pictures.

Word Box

高、矮、胖、瘦、多、少、肉、人口、照片、好吃、旅游、篮球、足球、蔬菜(shūcài vegetable)、辣(là spicy)、专业(zhuānyè major)

☼ 如果有不知道的词语，你可以问问老师或同学，也可以查阅书后面的词汇表。
Ask your teacher or lookup new words in the Vocabulary Index at the end of the textbook when you encounter them.

4. 两人一组，和同伴一起说说图片的内容。
   Work in pairs and discuss the pictures.

   > 同伴说的时候，你应该注意听。如果有听不懂的地方，一定要问问他(她)。
   > **Listen to your partner carefully and ask him/her about things don't understand.**

5. 两人一组，和同伴一起根据图片内容回答下面的问题。
   Work in pairs and answer the following questions according to the pictures.

   (1) 山本的样子和他的同屋有什么不一样？

   (2) 他俩家里的人口都比较多吗？

   (3) 他们俩学习的专业是什么？

   (4) 他们俩爱吃的东西一样吗？

   (5) 他们俩有什么共同(gòngtóng common)的爱好？

   (6) 他们有什么不同的爱好？

   > ●给老师的提示：这一题您可以带着全班一起完成。只要内容正确即可。

二、语言形式 Language Focus (约20分钟)

1. 和同伴一起复习下面的语言形式和例句，然后每个人用不同的语言表达形式说一个新句子。
   Work with your partner to review the following structures and example sentences. Each says a new sentence with each structure.

   ● ……比…… +（形容词/动词）：

   我觉得，吃蔬菜比吃肉好。
   我们一起开始学习汉语，他比我学得好。
   我九月刚来中国，他比我早一年，已经学了一年了。

   ● ……比…… +（形容词）+ 一些/得多/多了：

   他打篮球打得比我好多了。

   ● ……不如…… +（形容词/动词）：

   我打篮球不如他，因为他比我高。
   姐姐不如我爱吃甜食。

16

2. 写出16页热身活动第5题中那6个问题的答案。试着用一用上面表示比较的语言形式。

Write answers to the 6 questions in the No.5 of Warm-Up section on page 16. Try to use the comparative structures above.

(1)

(2)

(3)

(4)

(5)

(6)

●给老师的提示：
这一题您可以采取先写后说的方式进行，并指导学生选择更好的表达方式。

写作任务 Writing Task

一、 组织材料 Organizing Materials (约20分钟)

1. 阅读课文，并回答问题。
   Read the text and answer the questions.

我 和 我 的同屋

　　我是日本留学生山本一郎，来中国快半年了。我刚来的时候一句汉语也不会说，学习和生活都有很多困难。我的同屋马丁经常帮助我，现在我们已经是好朋友了。我们虽然是好朋友，但是我们俩在很多方面都不一样。

　　马丁是美国人，从小就对中国的历史和文化感兴趣，他是去年9月来中国的，比我早一年，汉语也比我学得好，现在已经开始学习他的专业——中国历史了。

　　马丁的个子比我高得多，篮球打得很好。可是我不喜欢打篮球，我喜欢踢足球。我们经常一起去饭馆吃饭。马丁爱吃肉，还喜欢吃辣的；我爱吃蔬菜，不爱吃辣的，所以我们就自己点自己喜欢吃的菜。

　　我们俩都喜欢旅行。周末我们经常和朋友们一起去郊区爬山，去公园照相。我们打算放假的时候一起去云南 (Yúnnán a province of China)旅行，听说那儿是中国少数民族(mínzú minorities)最多的地方，风景也很美。

(1) 山本来中国以前学过汉语吗？

(2) 马丁和山本谁学汉语学得好？

(3) 马丁的专业是什么？他为什么学这个专业？

(4) 山本和马丁有什么不同？

(5) 放假时他们打算去哪儿旅行？为什么？

● 给老师的提示：这一题您可以带着全班一起完成。并请您参考书后面的"汉语常用标点符号一览表"，提醒学生注意破折号和分号的用法。

2. 和同伴一起说说，山本从哪些方面介绍了自己和马丁的情况。写出3个最重要的方面。
Talk with your partner about which aspects Yamamoto introduces about himself and Martin. Write the three most important aspects.

(1)

(2)

(3)

3. 想一想你的同屋（朋友），在下面的表格中写出你和你的同屋（朋友）有什么相同点，有什么不同点。

Think about your roommateor friend. Fill in the table with the similarities and differences between you and your roommate or friend.

内容 Content	相同点 Similarities	不同点 Diferences
基本情况(年龄、国籍等) Basic Information (Age, Nationality, etc.)		
外表(身高、胖瘦等) Appearance (Height, Body Type, etc.)		
兴趣爱好 Interests and Hobbies		
饮食习惯 Eating Habits		
其他 Others		

☀ 只写出重要的词语或句子就可以了，不用写得太多。
Write down key words or sentences.
You do not need to write too much.

4. 想一想可以从哪些方面介绍你的同屋。将你认为最重要的4个方面写在下面。

Think about how to introduce your roommate. Write the four most important aspects below.

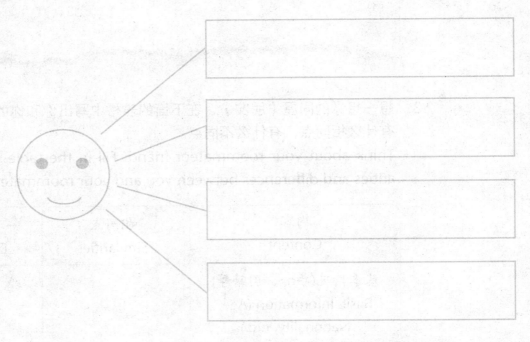

☀ 不会写的字，先用拼音写。

If there are any characters that you cannot write, you may write them in Pinyin first.

二、动手写 Getting It Down (约20分钟)

请你用20分钟写一段话，介绍一下你的同屋或朋友。

In 20 minutes, write a paragraph introducing your roommate or friend.

◉ 要注意通过和自己比较来突出
他(她)的特点。

Pay attention to stress his/her characteristics by comparison with yourself.

◉ 请你参考课文的格式写。不会写的
字，可以先用拼音写。

Refer to the form of the text. If there are any characters that you cannot write, you may write them in Pinyin first.

讨论修改 Discussion and Revision (约10分钟)

1. 与同伴交换所写的短文，看后回答问题。
   Exchange paragraphs with your partner and then answer the following questions.

(1) 你的同伴是从哪几个方面介绍他(她)的同屋(朋友)的？
   From which aspects did your partner introduces his/her roommate or friend?

(2) 他(她)的同屋(朋友)和他(她)有什么不同？
   What differences are there between his/her roommate or friend and him/her?

(3) 你觉得他(她)介绍得清楚吗？你还想知道什么？

Do you think he/she clearly made the introduction? What else do you want to know?

(4) 你的同伴有没有写错字？有的话就告诉他(她)。

Are there any wrong characters? If there are, tell him/her.

(5) 如果有你不知道的词和不认识的字，就问问他(她)。

Are there any characters and words that you do not recognize? If there are, ask him/her.

(6) 看看短文的格式对不对，如果不对就告诉他(她)。

Check whether your partner used the correct form. If there are any mistakes, tell him/her.

(7) 看看短文中的"，"和"。"是不是写成"、"或者"."了。

Check whether "，" and "。" are written as "、" or "." in his/her paragraph.

◈ 互相检查，改正错误，遇到困难可以问老师。

Check what your partner wrote and correct the errors. Ask your teacher when you encounter difficulties.

2. 改正自己短文中的错误，然后和其他小组交流一下。

Correct the errors in your paragraph and then share with other groups.

●给老师的提示：您可以请几个学生朗读他们的文章，使同学们分享彼此的写作成果。您还可以从学生的文章中总结一些实用的结构写在黑板上，最后做些简单、必要的讲解，作为本课的总结。

二、补充提高 Growing and Improving

1. 对你写的短文再进行一次补充和修改，然后抄写在作业本上交给老师批改。

   Revise the paragraph again and add the new content. Rewrite your paragraph and hand it in to your teacher.

2. 如果有时间，你可以写一篇短文介绍一下你的老师。

   If time permits, write a short paragraph introducing your teacher.

要注意充分利用这一课所学的新词、新结构等，并尽量吸取其他同学文章中的成功之处。

Make use of the new words, structures, etc. in this lesson, and try your best to absorb the strong points from what your classmates wrote.

3

买旗袍

学习简单叙述购物经历

Learn to narrate a shopping experience

写前准备 Before Writing

一、热身活动 Warm-Up (约30分钟)

1. 看看下面的图片，从小词库里选择词语写在合适的图片下边。
   Look at the following pictures and then write the words from the Word Box under the appropriate pictures.

Word Box

老板、价钱、便宜、贵、试、旗袍(qípáo cheongsam)、砍价(kǎnjià to bargain)、镜子(jìngzi mirror)、服装摊儿(fúzhuāng tānr clothes stall)、讨价还价(tǎo jià huán jià)

* 除了小词库里的词语以外，你还想起了什么词，也可以写在图片的下边。

Besides the words in the Word Box, write down ideas that come to you next to the pictures.

2. 两人一组，看看你和同伴写的词语一样不一样，然后一起说说图片的内容。

Work in pairs. Look at whether the words you wrote are the same as your partner's, and then talk about the pictures together.

> 同伴说的时候，你应该注意听。如果有不知道的词语，一定要问问他(她)。
>
> Listen to your partner carefully and ask him/her about the things you don't understand.

3. 请在图片的旁边为每一幅图片写几句话，简单叙述一下图片的内容。

Write several sentences next to each pictures to narrate the picture story.

> 不会写的字，可以先用拼音写。
>
> If there are any characters that you cannot write, you may write them in *Pinyin* first.

● 给老师的提示：这一题您可以采取先写后说的方式进行。

二、语言形式 Language Focus (约20分钟)

1. 和同伴一起看看下面的例句，复习能愿动词。

Work with your partner to see the following example sentences and review the modal particles.

● "要"、"想"、"愿意"等主要表示意愿。例如：

   "要"，"想"，"愿意" etc. indicate willingness. E.g.

   天气冷了，我要出去买一件大衣。
   她想把窗户关上，可是同屋不愿意。
   安娜不愿意住在学校，在外面租了一套房子。

● "应该"、"得(děi)"等表示对情理、事理的判断。例如：

   "应该"，"得(děi)" etc. indicate judgments over matters. E.g.

   天气冷了，你应该买一件大衣。
   他不认识路，我一定得陪他去。

● "能"、"可以"等表示对主客观条件的判断。例如：
"能"，"可以" etc. indicate judgments over subjective and objective conditions. E.g.

所有的学生都能在这个图书馆借书。
明天下午有事，你不可以上街买东西。

● "可能"、"会"、"能"等表示可能。例如：
"可能"，"会"，"能" etc. indicate possibilities. E.g.

雨下得这么大，大卫可能不会来了。
如果你不吃，他一个人会把所有的东西都吃了。
这个饺子不大，20个饺子我能吃完。

2. 请你再看看图1到图6，试着根据图片内容用能愿动词写3个句子。
Look at the pictures 1–6 again. Try to write three sentences with modal particles according to the pictures.

●给老师的提示：
这两题您可以采取先写后说的方式进行，并指导学生表达得更准确。

(1)

(2)

(3)

写作任务　Writing Task

一、组织材料　Organizing Materials （约20分钟）

1. 你在中国的市场里买过什么东西吗？请简单填写一下表格。
Have you bought anything in Chinese markets? Briefly fill in the table below.

你买过的东西 Items You Bought	东西的价钱 Items' Prices	买东西的市场 Markets

2. 两人一组，给同伴介绍一下你在中国买东西的一次经历。
   Work in pairs and talk to your partner about your shopping experience in China.

3. 阅读课文，并回答问题。
   Read the text and answer the questions.

买 旗 袍

　　安娜一直想买一件旗袍，但是她没有那么多钱，所以打算买一件便宜的，150元左右就行。

　　大商场里的旗袍都非常贵，而且不能砍价，所以安娜来到了一个服装市场。听说这里的旗袍比商场便宜得多，安娜很高兴。一进市场安娜就看上了一件旗袍，颜色和样子都不错，可是价钱是380元，太贵了！

　　安娜在市场里转了半天，终于又看到了同样的旗袍。这个老板告诉她220元一件，喜欢的话可以试穿。安娜决定在这儿试一试，因为比刚才便宜了很多。她试衣服的时候，老板夸(kuā to praise)她穿旗袍很漂亮，劝(quàn to persuade)她买一件。安娜一边照镜子一边说："便宜一点儿可以吗？"老板说："当然可以。你说多少钱吧！"安娜说："140怎么样？"可是老板不同意，她要160元。安娜喜欢这件衣服，而且160元的价钱也不贵，于是她就买了一件。

　　安娜今天很高兴，因为她买到了喜欢的衣服，而且用汉语砍价也非常成功。

(1) 安娜为什么想买一件便宜的旗袍？

(2) 安娜为什么去服装市场？

(3) 第一个老板说"380元"，安娜为什么不砍价？

(4) 安娜为什么在第二个老板那儿买了旗袍？

(5) 今天安娜为什么很高兴？

●给老师的提示：这一题您可以带着全班一起完成。并请您参考书后面的"汉语常用标点符号一览表"，提醒学生注意冒号和引号的用法。

4. 根据你买东西的一次经历，利用下面的问题整理你的思路。
Use the following questions to gather your thoughts about one of your shopping experiences.

(1) 你那次买东西是什么时候？

(2) 那天你为什么要上街？

(3) 那天你为什么想买这个东西？

(4) 你为什么没在别的商场买？

(5) 老板一开始说的价钱是多少？你听了以后怎么想的？

(6) 最后你是多少钱买的？

(7) 东西的质量怎么样？买了以后你后悔了吗？

●给老师的提示：这一题是帮助学生确定写作内容和写作顺序的，所以，您可以引导学生抓住重点把事情说清楚。

二、动手写 Getting It Down (约20分钟)

请你用20分钟写一段话，叙述那一次你买东西的经历。
In 20 minutes, write a paragraph to narrate that shopping experience.

※ 请你参考课文的格式写。不会写的字，可以先用拼音写。
Refer to the form of the text. If there are any characters that you cannot write, you may write them in *Pinyin* first.

讨论修改 Discussion and Revision （约20分钟）

1. 与同伴交换所写的短文，看后回答问题。
   Exchange paragraphs with your partner and then answer the following questions.

(1) 他(她)写的句子你都能看懂吗？把看不懂的句子画出来，告诉他(她)。

   Do you understand everything your partner wrote? Mark the unclear sentences and ask him/her.

(2) 他(她)买东西的经历写清楚了吗？不清楚的话，你可以问问他(她)。

Do you think his/her narration about the shopping experience is clear? If there is something unclear, ask him/her.

(3) 你的同伴写的这件事情发生在什么时候？什么地方？
When and where did it happen?

(4) 你的同伴有没有写错字？有的话就告诉他(她)。
Are there any wrong characters? If there are, tell him/her.

(5) 如果有你不知道的词和不认识的字，就问问他(她)。
If there are any characters you do not recognize, ask him/her.

(6) 看看短文的格式对不对，如果不对就告诉他(她)。
Check whether your partner used the correct form. If there are any mistakes, tell him/her.

(7) 看看短文中的"，"和"。"是不是写成"、"或者"."了。
Check whether "," and "。" are written as "、" or "." in his/her paragraph.

◎ 互相检查，改正错误，遇到困难可以问老师。
Check what your partner wrote and correct the errors. Ask your teacher when you encounter difficulties.

2. 改正自己短文中的错误，然后和其他小组交流一下。
Correct the errors in your paragraph and then discuss with other groups.

● 给老师的提示：您可以请几个学生朗读他们的文章，使同学们分享彼此的写作成果。您还可以从学生的文章中总结一些实用的结构写在黑板上，最后做些简单、必要的讲解，作为本课的总结。

作 业　Assignment

一、复习整理 Review

1. 整理本课所写过的句子和短文，把错句、错字改正后写在下边。

   Review the sentences and paragraphs you wrote in this lesson, and correct the sentences and characters which were written incorrectly.

2. 整理本课所写过的句子和短文，将生词和新的结构找出来，写在下边，还可以用它们写几个新的句子，帮助自己记忆。

   Review the sentences and paragraphs you wrote in this lesson. Pick out the new words and structures and write them down. Make some new sentences with them to help you memorize them.

二、补充提高 Growing and Improving

1. 对你写的短文再进行一次补充和修改，然后抄写在作业本上交给老师批改。

   Revise the paragraph again and add the new content. Rewrite your paragraph and hand it in to your teacher.

2. 写一篇短文，说说你和朋友一起去饭馆吃饭的经历。

   Write a paragraph narrating an experience in which you and your friend dined at a restaurant.

   ❋ 要注意充分利用你在这一课学习的所有新词、新结构等，并尽量吸取其他同学文章中的成功之处。

   Make use of the new words, structures, etc. in this lesson, and try your best to absorb the strong points from what your classmates wrote.

这套房子真漂亮

学习比较和评价事物的特点
Learn to compare and evaluate the characteristics of things

写前准备 Before Writing

一、 热身活动 Warm-Up (约30分钟)

1. 仔细看看下面的图片，然后从小词库里选择词语写在合适的图片下边。
Look at the following pictures, and then write the words from the Word Box under the appropriate pictures.

院子、厕所、介绍、脏、干净、旧、新、钥匙、房租(fángzū rent)、合租(hézū to rent together with somebody else)、租(zū to rent)、同屋(tóng wū roommate)、卫生间(wèishēngjiān toilet)、客厅(kètīng living room)、卧室(wòshì bedroom)

☀如果有不知道的词语，你可以问问老师或同学，也可以查阅书后面的词汇表。
Ask your teacher or look up the new words in the Vocabulary Index at the end of the textbook when you encounter them.

2. 两人一组，和同伴一起说说图片的内容。请尽量使用你写在图片下边的词语。
Work in pairs and discuss the pictures. Try your best to use the words next to the pictures.

☀同伴说的时候，你应该注意听。如果有听不懂的地方，一定要问问他(她)。
Listen to your partner carefully and ask him/her about things you don't understand.

3. 假如你也在场，你想问安娜什么问题？请你把问题写在下面。
Suppose that you were present too. What do you want to ask Anna? Write your questions below.

4. 给同伴读一读你写的问题，看看你们想问安娜的问题有什么不一样。
Read the questions you wrote to your partner. See whether the questions you want to ask Anna are the same as your partner's.

●给老师的提示：您可以请几个学生说一说他们写的句子，看看大家一共有多少个问题想问安娜。

5. 再看看图片，和你的同伴一起回答下面的问题，然后针对每一个问题在下面写出3个重要的词语。

Look at the pictures again. Work in pairs to answer the following questions, and then write three key words to each question.

(1) 安娜想租一套什么样的房子？

_____

(2) 她喜欢第一套房子吗？为什么？

_____

(3) 她对第二套房子满意吗？为什么？

_____

(4) 第三套房子怎么样？安娜觉得有什么问题？

_____

(5) 安娜为什么和朋友一起租房子？

_____

※ 只写重要的词语，不要写句子。
Write key words instead of sentences.

二、语言形式 Language Focus (约20分钟)

1. 和同伴一起看看下面的例句，复习下面的关联词语。
Work with your partner to review the following example sentences and conjuncture particles.

- 既……又……：这个房间里既有电话，又有电视。
- 虽然……但是……：这个房间虽然很大，但是房间里什么东西都没有。
- 因为……所以……：因为我没有那么多钱，所以只能租一套小房子。
- 有……，有……，还有……：公园里有山，有水，还有很多树。
- 如果……就……：如果能跟你一起去上海就好了。

2. 写出热身活动第5题中那5个问题的答案，试着用一用上面的关联词语。

Write answers to the 5 questions in the No.5 of Warm-Up section on page 39. Try to use the comparative structures above.

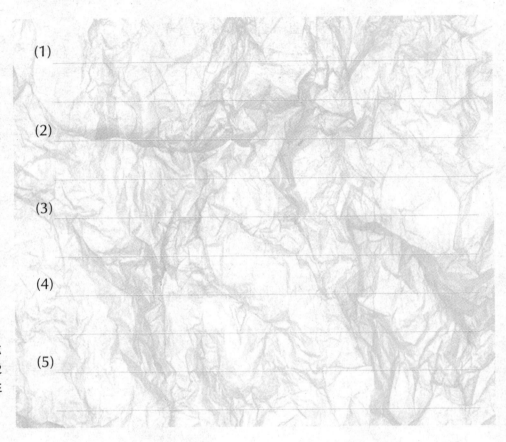

(1) _____

(2) _____

(3) _____

(4) _____

(5) _____

●给老师的提示：这一题您可以采取先说后写的方式带着全班学生一起完成。

3. 和同伴一起看看下面的例句，用"比"和"没有"说几个句子。

Work with your partner to see the following example sentences and say several sentences with "比" and "没有".

● 比：三班的教室比我们的（教室）大。
● 没有：大卫的房间没有我的（房间）干净。

4. 写3句话比较一下安娜看过的3套房子，试着用一用"比"和"没有"。

Write three sentences comparing the three apartments Anna saw. Try to use "比" and "没有".

(1)

(2)

(3)

写作任务 Writing Task

一、组织材料 Organizing Materials (约20分钟)

1. 如果可以租房子的话，你希望租一套什么样的房子？把你想到的重要词语写在下面。

Suppose that you wanted to rent an apartment. What kind of apartment would you prefer? Write down the key words that come to you.

● 不会写的字，可以先用拼音写。

If there are any characters that you cannot write, you may write them in *Pinyin* first.

2. 三人一组，轮流给同伴们介绍自己想租什么样的房子，并说明原因。每个听的人必须向说的人提出一个有关房子的问题。

Work in a group of three. Take turns to describe the apartment you like and explain the reasons. Each listener should ask a question about the apartment.

◎ 说的人要尽量回答每个人的问题。
The speaker should try to answer all the questions.

3. 阅读课文，并回答问题。

Read the text and answer the questions.

安娜租房子

　　安娜现在住在留学生公寓，可是她觉得跟中国人交流的机会比较少，所以她想在学校外面租一套价格合适的房子，那样的话她可以经常跟中国人用汉语交谈。于是她找到了一家中介公司(Zhōngjiè gōngsī an agent)。

　　中介公司的小张带着安娜看了三套房子。第一套房子虽然房租比较便宜，但是房子太旧了，而且又小又脏，安娜不满意。第二套房子在一个四合院(sìhéyuàn a compound with houses around a square courtyard)里，房间比第一套房子大，可是没有卫生间，厕所在院子里。住在这里虽然和中国人说话的机会非常多，但没有第一套房子方便。小张又带安娜看了第三套房子，这套房子又宽敞(kuānchang spacious)又漂亮，安娜一看就喜欢。房子里有客厅、有厨房和卫生间，还有两间卧室，但是房租也比第一套和第二套高多了。安娜一个人租的话太贵了，所以她得找一个同屋。

　　第二天安娜给中介公司打了个电话，她决定和法国留学生白姗合租这套房子。这样安娜既能住上漂亮的大房子，又不用交那么多房租。

(1) 安娜为什么要租房子？

(2) 她想租什么样的房子？

(3) 她看的前两套房子各有什么问题？

(4) 最后她租的那一套是什么样的房子？

(5) 你觉得安娜满意吗？为什么？

●给老师的提示：这一题您可以带着全班一起完成。

4. 按照下面的问题，整理一下你的思路。
Put your thoughts together according to the following questions.

(1) 你现在住的房子好不好？为什么？

(2) 在学生公寓住有什么利弊(lìbì advantages and disadvantages)？

(3) 在校外租房子有什么利弊？

(4) 如果有机会租房子，你想租一间什么样的房子？为什么？

二、动手写 Getting It Down (约20分钟)

请你用20分钟写一段话，比较一下在学生公寓住和在校外租房子住各有什么利弊。

In 20 minutes, write a paragraph to compare the advantages and disadvantages between living in a student dormitory versus an apartment outside the campus.

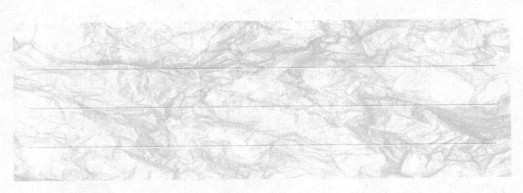

⊙ 请你参考课文的格式写。不会写的字，可以先用拼音写。

Refer to the form of the text. If there are any characters that you cannot write, you may write them in Pinyin first.

讨论修改 Discussion and Revision (约10分钟)

1. 与同伴交换所写的短文，看后回答问题。
   Exchange paragraphs with your partner and then answer the following questions.

   (1) 你的同伴想租房子吗？
   Does your partner want to rent an apartment?

   (2) 他(她)喜欢的房子是什么样的？找出他(她)写的句子。
   What kind of apartments does he/she like? Find out his/her answers.

   (3) 找出他(她)写的租房的好处，看看你们俩的看法一样不一样。
   Find out the advantages of renting an apartment that he/she wrote. See whether your opinions are the same as your partner's.

   (4) 你的同伴有没有写错字？有的话就告诉他(她)。
   Are there any wrong characters? If there are, tell him/her.

   (5) 如果有你不知道的词和不认识的字，就问问他(她)。
   If there are any characters you do not recognize, ask him/her.

(6) 看看短文的格式对不对，如果不对就告诉他(她)。
Check whether your partner used the correct form. If there are any mistakes, tell him/her.

(7) 看看短文中的"，"和"。"是不是写成"、"或者"."了。
Check whether "," and "。" are written as "、" or "." in his/her paragraph.

> ※ 互相检查，改正错误，遇到困难可以问老师。
> Check what your partner wrote and correct the errors. Ask your teacher when you encounter difficulties.

2. 改正自己短文中的错误，然后和其他小组交流一下。
Correct the errors in your paragraph and then discuss with other groups.

> ● 给老师的提示：您可以请几个学生朗读他们的文章，使同学们分享彼此的写作成果。您还可以从学生的文章中总结一些实用的结构写在黑板上，最后做些简单、必要的讲解，作为本课的总结。

作业 Assignment

一、复习整理 Review

1. 整理本课所写过的句子和短文，把错句、错字改正后写在下边。
Review the sentences and paragraphs you wrote in this lesson, and correct the sentences and characters which were written incorrectly.

2. 整理本课所写过的句子和短文，将生词和新的结构找出来，写在下边，还可以用它们写几个新的句子，帮助自己记忆。
Review the sentences and paragraphs you wrote in this lesson. Pick out the new words and structures and write them down. Make some new sentences with them to help you memorize them.

二、补充提高 Growing and Improving

1. 对你写的短文再进行一次补充和修改，然后抄写在作业本上交给老师批改。

   Revise the paragraph again and add the new content. Rewrite your paragraph and hand it in to your teacher.

2. 写一篇短文比较一下你在中国住的房间和你在自己的国家住的房间。

   Write a paragraph to compare the place you live in China with that in your own contry.

> ✿ 要注意充分利用你在这一课学习的所有新词、新结构等，并尽量吸取其他同学文章中的成功之处。
>
> *Make use of the new words, structures, etc. in this lesson, and try your best to absorb the strong points from what your classmates wrote.*

这里的天气真好

学习目标 Objective

学习简单说明一般的天气情况和天气变化

Learn to explain common weather conditions and variations

5

写前准备　Before Writing

一、热身活动　Warm-Up（约30分钟）

1. 你知道哪些有关天气的词语？把你想到的词语写在下面的小词库里。
   Which words do you know about weather? Write the words that come to you below.

● 不会写的字，可以用拼音写。
If there are any characters that you cannot write, you may write them in Pinyin.

2. 两人一组，和同伴一起说说春、夏、秋、冬四个季节的天气有什么不同。
   Work in pairs. Discuss the different weather conditions of spring, summer, autumn and winter.

● 给老师的提示：您可以请几个学生分别说说每一个季节的天气，并有意识地为他们补充一些有关天气的词语。

3. 仔细看看下面的图片，然后从小词库里选择词语写在合适的图片下边。
   Look at the following pictures, and then write the words from the Word Box under the appropriate pictures.

如果有不知道的词语，你可以问问老师或同学，也可以查阅书后面的词汇表。
Ask your teacher or look up the new words in the Vocabulary Index at the end of the textbook when you encounter them.

告别、车票、地图、毛衣、脱、手机、火车站、外套
(wàitào coat)、单衣(dānyī unlined clothes)、毛背心
(máo bèixīn a sleeveless woolen waistcoat)、候车室
(hòuchē shì waiting room) 树叶 (shùyè leaf)、旅行包
(lǚxíng bāo suitcase)、站台(zhàntái railway platform)

幸子去香港旅行

4. 两人一组，和同伴一起说说图片的内容。
Work in pairs and discuss the pictures.

☀ 同伴说的时候，你应该注意听。如果有听不懂的地方，一定要问问他(她)。
Listen to your partner carefully and ask him/her about things you don't understand.

5. 读一读下面的句子，然后把合适的句子抄写在相关的图片旁边。
Read the following sentences and write the appropriate sentences next to the related pictures.

(1) 幸子穿着衬衫和毛背心，背着旅行包，一手拿着大外套，一手拿着手机，走出了香港火车站。

(2) 火车停在一个小站上，幸子买东西的时候看到车站上的人都穿着毛衣，站台上的树是绿的，还有很多漂亮的花。

(3) 幸子收到了山本的短信，山本想知道天气怎么样。

(4) 冬天放寒假了，幸子要去旅行。她穿着大外套，背着旅行包正在和山本告别。

(5) 来到火车站时，时间还早，所以幸子坐在候车室里看地图。她发现香港离北京真的很远。

二、语言形式 Language Focus (约20分钟)

1. 和同伴一起看看下面的例句，然后每个人用不同的语言表达形式说一个新句子。
   Work with your partner to review the following example sentences, and then each says a new sentence using each structure.

   - "越来越……"表示程度随着时间发展变化。例如：
     "越来越……" indicates change of degree as time goes by. E.g.

     冬天到了，北京的天气越来越冷，人们穿的衣服也越来越厚。
     我的汉语水平越来越高，中国人说的话我差不多都听懂了。

   - "越……越……"表示程度上后者随着前者增加而增加。例如：
     "越……越……" indicates the increase in degree of the latter with that of the former. E.g.

     雨越下越大了，我们赶快回去吧。
     听说越往南方走，天气越暖和。

2. 请你替幸子给山本回一个短信，告诉她一路上的天气变化。试着用一用"越来越……"或者"越……越……"。
   Send a reply text message to Yamamoto for Sachiko, telling her the weather variation on the trip, and try to use "越来越……".

   幸子给山本回的短信

3. 和同伴一起看看下面的例句，复习一下时量补语。每个人说几个新句子。
Work with your partner to review the following example sentences and the time-measure complements. Each says several new sentences.

注意时量补语在句子中的位置：

● 时量补语用在动词的后面，表示动作或者状态持续时间的长短。
例如：

Time-measure complements should be used after verbs indicating the duration of an action or a state. E.g.

这一场雨下了三天三夜。
天只阴了一会儿就出太阳了。
安娜坐火车坐了20多个小时。

●给老师的提示：这一题您可以采取先写后说的方式进行，并指导学生表达得更准确。

写作任务 Writing Task

一、组织材料 Organizing Materials (约20分钟)

1. 你觉得最近一段时间天气怎么样？和前一段时间比发生了什么变化？把你想到的重要的词语或句子写在下面。
How is the weather recently? What changes have taken place recently? Write the key words and sentences that come to you below.

◎ 不会写的字，可以先用拼音写。
If there are any characters that you cannot write, you may write them in Pinyin first.

2. 两人一组，和你的同伴交换一下看法，看看你们的想法有什么不同，并说明原因。

Work in pairs. Share your ideas with your partner. Identify what differences in opinion between you and your partner and explain the reasons.

3. 阅读课文，并回答问题。

Read the text and answer the questions.

幸子去香港旅行

北京的天气越来越冷，校园里不但没有花了，连树叶也掉光了。

放寒假了，幸子今天要去香港旅行。她穿着一件大外套，背着一个大旅行包出发了。她来到火车站，时间还早，所以就坐在候车室里看地图。幸子看到香港在中国的南边，离北京很远。

幸子在火车上睡了一夜，早上火车停在一个小站上。幸子下车买东西的时候看到：站台上的树都是绿的，还有很多漂亮的花，人们也只穿着一件毛衣。而且，越走天气越热。到了香港，幸子只能拿着大外套，穿着衬衫和毛背心出站。坐了20多个小时的火车，幸子又换上了春天的衣服。

幸子刚一出香港站，她的手机就响了，是山本的短信。山本问她天气怎么样，幸子在短信中告诉他：一路上天气越来越热，到了香港感觉就像春天，一点儿也不冷。

(1) 现在北京是什么季节？为什么？

(2) 幸子要去哪儿旅行？她出发时穿着什么衣服？

(3) 幸子在地图上的什么地方找到了香港？

(4) 在火车上的第二天早上，幸子感觉到了什么变化？

(5) 到了香港，幸子身上的衣服有什么变化？

●给老师的提示：这一题您可以带着全班一起完成。

4. 利用下面的问题，整理一下思路。

Use the following questions to put your thoughts together.

问 题	你 的 看 法
你喜欢哪一个季节？为什么？	
现在是什么季节？	
这几天天气怎么样？有什么变化？	
这个季节的天气和上一个季节有什么不同？	

⊙ 只写出重要的词语或句子就可以了，不用写得太多。

Just write the key words and sentences. You don't need to write too much.

二、动手写 Getting It Down (约20分钟)

请你用20分钟写一段话，介绍一下这个季节的气候特点和最近的天气变化。

In 20 minutes, write a paragraph to introduce the climate characteristics of this season and the recent weather variations.

⊙ 不会写的字，可以先用拼音写。

If there are any characters that you cannot write, you may write them in Pinyin first.

讨论修改 Discussion and Revision (约10分钟)

1. 与同伴交换所写的短文，看后回答问题。
   Exchange paragraphs with your partner and then answer the following questions.

   (1) 你的同伴在短文中都写了什么内容？
   What did your partner write?

   (2) 你能知道他(她)喜欢什么样的天气吗？
   Can you tell what kind of weather your partner prefers?

   (3) 他(她)喜欢哪一个季节？为什么？
   What season does he/she prefer? Why?

   (4) 你的同伴有没有写错字？有的话就告诉他(她)。
   Are there any wrong characters? If there are, tell him/her.

   (5) 如果有你不知道的词和不认识的字，就问问他(她)。
   If there are any characters you do not recognize, ask him/her.

   (6) 看看短文的格式对不对，如果不对就告诉他(她)。
   Check whether your partner used the correct form. If there are any mistakes, tell him/her.

   (7) 看看短文中的"，"和"。"是不是写成"、"或者"."了。
   Check whether "," and "。" are written as "、" or "." in his/her paragraph.

   ❋ 互相检查，改正错误，遇到困难可以问老师。
   Check what your partner wrote and correct the errors. Ask your teacher when you encounter difficulties.

2. 改正自己短文中的错误，然后和其他小组交流一下。

Correct the errors in your paragraph and then discuss with other groups.

●给老师的提示：您可以请几个学生朗读他们的文章，使同学们分享彼此的写作成果。您还可以从学生的文章中总结一些实用的结构写在黑板上，最后做些简单、必要的讲解，作为本课的总结。

一、 复习整理 Review

1. 整理本课所写过的句子和短文，把错句、错字改正后写在下边。

Review the sentences and paragraphs you wrote in this lesson, and correct the sentences and characters which were written incorrectly.

2. 整理本课所写过的句子和短文，将生词和新的结构找出来，写在下边，还可以用它们写几个新的句子，帮助自己记忆。

Review the sentences and paragraphs you wrote in this lesson. Pick out the new words and structures and write them down. Make some new sentences with them to help you memorize them.

二、补充提高 Growing and Improving

1. 对你写的短文再进行一次补充和修改，然后抄写在作业本上交给老师批改。

Revise the paragraph again and add the new content. Rewrite your paragraph and hand it in to your teacher.

2. 写一篇短文介绍一下你们国家不同季节的天气情况。

Write a paragraph to introduce the weather conditions of various seasons in your country.

❀ 要注意充分利用你在这一课学习的所有新词、新结构等，并尽量吸取其他同学文章中的成功之处。

Make use of the new words, structures, etc. in this lesson, and try your best to absorb the strong points from what your classmates wrote.

复习（一）

按自测问题选择或填写。
Choose or fill in the form according to the self-test questions.

自测问题 Self-Test Questions	试着选择或写出你的答案 Choose or Write the Answers
1. 你现在能写一般的留言条了吗？ Can you write a note?	A 能　B 还可以　C 不能
2. 你能简单介绍一个人的特点了吗？ Can you introduce a person's characteristics?	A 能　B 还可以　C 不能
3. 请你试着写出一些可以说明人的特点的词语。 Write some words describing a person's characteristics.	高…… 喜欢……
4. 你能简单叙述自己的购物经历了吗？ Can you write a paragraph narrating one of your shopping experiences?	A 能　B 还可以　C 不能
5. 请试着写出一些与购物有关的词语。 Write some words relating to shopping.	贵…… 老板……
6. 你知道怎样简单比较和评价事物的特点了吗？ Do you know how to compare and evaluate the characteristics of things?	A 能　B 还可以　C 不能
7. 请你试着写出几个表示比较的词语。 Write some words relating to comparison.	比……

8. 请你试着写出一些可以说明和评价居室特点的词语。 Write some words relating to explaining and evaluating a room's characteristics.	大、干净……
9. 你能简单说明一般的天气情况和天气变化了吗？ Can you explain weather conditions and changes?	A 能　B 还可以　C 不能
10. 请你试着写出一些与天气有关的词语。 Write some words relating to the weather.	晴

二、复习与扩展　Review and Extension

1. 2~3人一组，找出下面两张留言条上的错误。
   Work in a groups of 2 or 3. Identify the errors in the following two notes.

> 李丽：
> 有个朋友突然来看我，所以我下午不能跟你一起去书店了。对不起。
> 　　　　　　　　　　　　　　　　　　朴美善

> 孙飞：
> 　　我今天来还你的CD，而且还想请你一起吃饭，可是你出去了，真遗憾。那么下次吧。另，你借给我的CD非常好听，我听了很多遍。谢谢！
> 　　　　　　　　　　　　　　　　　　马克
> 　　　　　　　　　　　　　　　　　　18, 10, 2006

遇到生词可以查词典，也可以问问老师。
Ask your teacher or use the dictionary when you encounter new words.

● 给老师的提示：学生做完后，您可以让各组说说答案，在全班交流一下。

2. 介绍一位你喜欢的名人。

   Introduce one of the famous people who you like.

   (1) 想一想你最喜欢的一位名人，在下面的表格中填写关于他(她)的信息。

   Think about one of the famous people who you like most and fill in the following table with his/her information.

项　目	内　容
姓名	
年龄	
出生地 Place of Birth	
职业 Occupation	
外貌特点 Appearance	
爱好	
主要经历 Experiences	例：他当过工人……
你对他(她)的评价 Evaluations	

   (2) 两人一组，利用表格中的信息给同伴介绍这位名人。

   Work in pairs. Use the information in the table to introduce the famous person.

   ❀ 你要说得有趣、生动一些，这样会让你的同伴对这位名人更感兴趣。

   Try to make your introduction interesting and vivid, so that it makes your partner interested in this famous people.

3. 想一想你在中国（或其他国家）去过的一个市场和你们国家的一个市场。

Think about a market you have been to in China (or another country) and one in your country.

(1) 两个国家的市场在下面3个方面的情况是怎样的？请根据实际情况写出你想到的词语。

How are the two markets in terms of the following three aspects? Write the words that come to you according to the actual situation.

	_____的市场	你们国家的市场
价格	便宜……	
环境	比较大……	
商品种类		

(2) 利用表格中的信息比较一下两个国家的市场。

Use the information in the table to compare the two markets.

例：在价格方面，中国的市场东西比较便宜。我们国家的市场东西贵一点儿，特别是水果，价钱比中国的贵多了。

比、没有……那么……、不如……那么……

❀ 小词库里的词语可以帮助你。

The words in the Word Box may help you.

在价格方面，_____

_____

在环境方面，_____

_____

在商品种类方面，_____

_____

三、写作工作室 Writing Workshop

全班一起出一期主题为"我的家"的墙报，每个同学为这个墙报写一段话。
Each student writes a paragraph for a special edition of wall newspaper to be titled My Family.

1. 这期墙报的内容可以分为以下几个方面的话题，请从中选择一个你比较感兴趣的话题。
   Choose a topic you are comparatively interested in from the following:

   ☐ 我的家人
   (介绍你的一位家人，包括外貌特点、爱好、经历、你对他[她]的评价等。Introduce one of your family members, including his/her appearance, hobbies, experiences, your evaluations, etc.)

   ☐ 我的家
   (介绍你家的房子和你家的特点。Introduce the place where you live and its characteristics.)

   ☐ 我们家乡的天气
   (介绍你们家乡的天气特点。Introduce the weather characteristics of your hometown.)

2. 与选择同一个话题的同学组成小组，坐在一起谈谈你自己想到的内容。
   Form groups according to the different topics and discuss what you think.

   > 要注意听别人讲，并互相提问题，使你们的介绍更清楚、更丰富。
   > Listen to your partners carefully and ask questions of each other, in order to make your introduction more clear and content-rich.

3. 大家分头准备自己的初稿，写好后互相检查修改。
   Each student prepares his/her own first draft. After finishing, check and revise each other's first draft.

4. 把修改过的稿子重新抄好，并找一些与你写的内容有关的照片、图片。
   Make a copy of the revised draft, and find some relevant photos and pictures.

5. 全班一起把所有材料按你们喜欢的形式在几张大一些的纸上布置好，然后贴在教室的墙上。
   As a group, work together to cut and paste all the materials onto a large piece of paper in a format you choose, and then paste it onto the wall in your classroom.

我的朋友病了

学习目标 Objective

学习说明常见病状及生病的原因

Learn to explain an illness and its causes

写前准备 Before Writing

一、热身活动 Warm-Up （约30分钟）

1. 看看图片旁边的词语，然后将词语与图片中对应的人体部位画线连接起来。
   Look at the words next to the picture, and then match them with the correct parts of the human body in the picture.

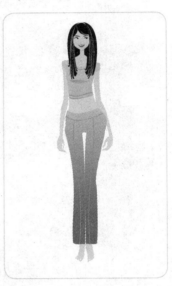

耳朵	ěrduo	ear
眼睛	yǎnjing	eye
肚子	dùzi	belly
头	tóu	head
嘴	zuǐ	mouth
胃	wèi	stomach
腰	yāo	waist
脚	jiǎo	foot
腿	tuǐ	leg

◉ 不知道的词语可以问问别人，也可以查阅书后面的词汇表。
Ask your teacher or look up the new words in the Vocabulary Index at the end of the textbook when you encounter them.

2. 两人一组，和同伴一起再补充一些你们知道的表示人体部位的词语。
   Work in pairs. Add more words about parts of the human body.

◉ 你应该想一想，除了上面给出的词语，你还知道哪些词语。
What words do you know apart from those given above?

3. 仔细看看下面的图片，然后从小词库里选择词语写在合适的图片下边。
    Look at the following pictures, and then write the words from the
    Word Box under the appropriate pictures.

Word Box

酒、疼、厕所、发烧、嗓子、流鼻涕(liú bítì to have
a runny nose)、打喷嚏(dǎ pēntì to sneeze)、拉肚子
(lā dùzi diarrhea)、恶心(ěxīn sick)、羊肉串(yáng ròu
chuàn lamb kebab)、下雨、冷

✦ 如果有不知道的词语，你可以问问老师或同学，也可以
查阅书后面的词汇表。
Ask your teacher or look up the new words in the Vocabulary
Index at the end of the textbook when you encounter them.

晚上12点   A-1

第二天早晨   A-2

4. 两人一组，和同伴一起说说图片的内容。
Work in pairs and discuss the pictures.

> 同伴说的时候，你应该注意听。如果有听不懂的地方，一定要问问他(她)。
> Listen to your partner carefully and ask him/her about things you don't understand.

5. 读一读下面的句子，然后把合适的句子抄写在相关的图片旁边。
Read the following sentences, and then write the appropriate sentences next to the pictures.

(1) 秋天已经到了，大家都穿上了毛衣，但是大卫觉得一点儿也不冷，所以穿得很少。可是他没想到突然下雨了。

(2) 金大成觉得羊肉串太好吃了，他不听朋友的劝告(quàngào to advise)，吃了很多。

(3) 因为老同学来了，山本特别高兴，一个人喝了10瓶啤酒。

(4) 早晨他的头特别疼，胃也特别疼，什么东西都不想吃，当然也不能去上课了。

(5) 他从夜里就开始拉肚子，到早晨的时候，他已经去了十几趟厕所了。他真后悔吃了那么多羊肉串。

(6) 大卫冻感冒了，又流鼻涕，又发烧，而且嗓子疼，头也疼，真是太难受(nánshòu uncomfortable)了。

二、语言形式 Language Focus (约20分钟)

1. 和同伴一起看看下面的例句，然后每个人用不同的语言表达形式说一个新句子。
Work with your partner to review the following example sentences, and then each says a new sentence using each structure.

● "一下儿"同"一下子"，表示某种动作发生、完成得快，或某种现象出现得突然，常与"就"一起用。例如：

"一下儿", the same as "一下子", indicates that an action happens and finishes quickly, or some phenomena appears suddenly. It is often used with "就". E.g.

他饿极了，一下儿就吃了一大盘饺子。
大雨过后，天气一下儿就冷了。
因为淋了大雨，他一下儿就感冒了。

● "一口气"表示动作是在很短的时间里连续完成的，和"一下儿"、"一下子"差不多。例如：

"一口气" suggests that an action takes place in a short time. Its usage is almost the same as "一下儿" and "一下子". E.g.

他一口气吃了三个大苹果。
他一口气说了好几个没来上课的原因。

2. 试着用"一下儿"、"一下子"或者"一口气"改写一下69页热身活动第5题中的第2、3、5这3个句子。

Try to use "一下儿", "一下子", or "一口气" to rewrite the 2nd, 3rd and 5th sentences in the No. 5 of the Warm-Up section on page 69.

(2)

(3)

(5)

☼ 你应该注意一下它们在句中的位置。
Pay attention to the position of the phrases in your sentences.

3. 和同伴一起看看下面的例句，复习反问句。
Work with your partner to review the rhetorical questions.

● 反问句是用反问的语气对于一个明显的道理或事实加以肯定或否定。句子里有否定词时强调一个肯定的意思；句子里没有否定词时强调一个否定的意思。例如：
A rhetorical question is to emphasize a positive or negative attitude to an obvious fact with a rhetorical mood. It stresses a positive meaning when there is negative term in the sentence; it stresses a negative meaning when no negative term in it. E.g.

你不是一点多才吃过午饭吗？现在当然不会饿。（你一点多才吃过午饭）

我没告诉你吗？小摊上的东西不能多吃。（我已经告诉你了）

老师早就通知过了，难道你不知道吗？（你应该知道）

我哪儿知道今天这么冷啊？（我不知道今天这么冷）

4. 请你再看看前面的3组图，根据图片内容试着写3个反问句。
Look at the three groups of pictures again. Write three rhetorical questions according to the pictures.

(1)

(2)

(3)

❀ 你应该注意不同的反问句所表示的不同意义。
Pay attention to the different meanings indicated by different rhetorical questions.

● 给老师的提示：这一题您可以采取先写后说的方式进行，并指导学生更好地表达。

71

写作任务　Writing Task

一、组织材料　Organizing Materials （约20分钟）

1. 你从小到大生过什么病？生病的时候有什么感觉？将你想到的词语写在下面的小词库里。

   What illnesses have you had since you were young? How did you feel when you were sick? Write the words that come to you below.

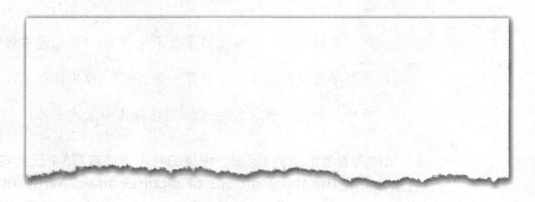

   ❀ 不会写的字，先用拼音写。

   If there are any characters that you cannot write, you may write them in Pinyin first.

2. 两人一组，给你的同伴讲一讲你生病时的情况，并说明一下生病的原因。

   Work in pairs to talk about the states you were ill and explain the causes of your illness.

   ❀ 同伴说的时候你要注意听，如果有听不懂的地方或是不知道的词语，一定要问一问他(她)。

   Listen to your partner carefully and ask him/her about things you don't understand.

3. 阅读课文，并回答问题。
Read the text and answer the questions.

我的朋友病了

　　秋天到了，天气也开始冷了，大部分同学都穿上了毛衣。我的朋友大卫身体特别好，他觉得一点儿也不冷，所以还一直穿着夏天的衣服和凉鞋(liángxié sandals)。

　　昨天我们一起去书店买书，去的时候天气挺好的，没想到回来的时候，下起了大雨，温度一下儿变得很低，大卫穿得那么少怎么能不冷呢？

　　第二天他没来上课。他感冒了。我去看他的时候，他正躺在床上，不停地流鼻涕、打喷嚏。他告诉我上午已经去医院看过病了，也吃了药。他嗓子疼，头也疼，还有些发烧，感到很难受。我觉得他好像瘦了很多。

(1) 现在是什么季节？天气怎么样？

(2) 大卫每天穿什么衣服？为什么？

(3) 大卫是怎么感冒的？

(4) 感冒有什么症状(zhèngzhuàng symptom)？

(5) 他有什么感觉？

●给老师的提示：这一题您可以带着全班一起完成。

4. 请按照下面的顺序，整理一下思路。
Put your thoughts together using the given order.

生病的人是：＿＿＿＿＿＿＿＿＿＿＿＿＿＿＿＿＿

生的病是：＿＿＿＿＿＿＿＿＿＿＿＿＿＿＿＿＿

生病的原因是：＿＿＿＿＿＿＿＿＿＿＿＿＿＿＿

这种病的症状是：＿＿＿＿＿＿＿＿＿＿＿＿＿＿

他(她)的感觉是：＿＿＿＿＿＿＿＿＿＿＿＿＿＿

※ 只写出重要的词语或句子就可以了，不需要写得太多。
Write key words or sentences only, you don't need to write too much.

二、动手写 Getting It Down （约20分钟）

请你用20分钟写一段话，介绍一下你自己或是一个你认识的人生病的事情。

In 20 minutes, write a paragraph to describe an illness that you or your acquaitance had.

◎ 不会写的字，可以先用拼音写。
If there are any characters that you cannot write, you may write them in *Pinyin* first.

写后修改 After Writing

1. 与同伴交换所写的短文，看后回答问题。
Exchange paragraphs with your partner and then answer the following questions.

(1) 你的同伴写的是谁生病的事情？
Whose illness did your partner write about?

☐他(她)自己　　☐他(她)的朋友　　☐他(她)的家人　　☐他(她)的同学

(2) 这件事情他(她)叙述得清楚吗？如果不清楚你可以告诉他(她)。
Do you think his/her description is clear? You may ask him/her about anything unclear.

(3) 这个病的症状他(她)都写出来了吗？
Did he/she write about all symptoms of the illness?

(4) 他(她)写的你都能看懂吗？你还想知道什么？
Do you understand everything your partner wrote? What else do you want to know?

(5) 你的同伴有没有写错字？有的话就告诉他(她)。
Are there any wrong characters? If there are, tell him/her.

(6) 如果有你不知道的词和不认识的字，你就问问他(她)。
If there are any characters you do not recognize, ask him/her.

(7) 短文中的标点符号都写对了吗？帮他(她)检查一下。
Are there any punctuation marks used incorrectly? Help him/her check them.

❋ 互相检查，改正错误，遇到困难可以问老师。
Check what your partner wrote and correct the errors.
Ask your teacher when you encounter difficulties.

2. 改正自己短文中的错误，然后和其他小组交流一下。
   Correct the errors in your paragraph and then discuss with other groups.

●给老师的提示：您可以请几个学生朗读他们的文章，使同学们分享彼此的写作成果。您还可以从学生的文章中总结一些实用的结构写在黑板上，最后做些简单、必要的讲解，作为本课的总结。

作业 Assignment

一、复习整理 Review

1. 整理本课所写过的句子和短文，把错句、错字改正后写在下边。
   Review the sentences and paragraphs you wrote in this lesson, and correct the sentences and characters which were written incorrectly.

2. 整理本课所写过的句子和短文，将生词和新的结构找出来，写在下边，
   还可以用它们写几个新的句子，帮助自己记忆。
   Review the sentences and paragraphs you wrote in this lesson. Pick out the new words and structures and write them down. Make some new sentences with them to help you memorize them.

二、 补充提高 Growing and Improving

1. 对你写的短文再进行一次补充和修改，然后抄写在作业本上交给老师批改。
   Revise the paragraph again and add the new content. Rewrite your paragraph and hand it in to your teacher.

2. 你害怕生病吗？写一段话说说为什么。
   Are you afraid of falling ill? Write a paragraph to explain your reasons.

   ◈ 要注意充分利用你在这一课学习的所有新词、新结构
   等，并尽量吸取其他同学文章中的成功之处。
   Make use of the new words, structures, etc. in this lesson, and try your best to absorb the strong points from what your classmates wrote.

7

今天真倒霉

学习目标 Objective

学习说明生活用品或设施的常见故障

Learn to explain basic breakdowns of supplies and facilities

写前准备 Before Writing

一、热身活动 Warm-Up (约30分钟)

1. 将下面的词语与对应的图片画线连接起来。
   Match the words with the pictures.

空调　　　　　　马桶　　　　　　电梯　　　　　　电灯　　　　　　电话
kōngtiáo　　　　mǎtǒng　　　　diàntī　　　　diàndēng　　　　diànhuà
air-conditioner　toilet　　　　elevator　　　　light　　　　　　telephone

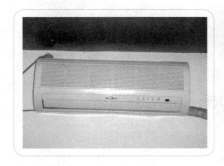 

☺ 不知道的词语可以问问别人，也可以查阅书后面的词汇表。
Ask your teacher or look up the new words in the Vocabulary Index at the end of the textbook when you encounter them.

2. 两人一组，和同伴一起说说，如果上面这些东西坏了，会出现什么情况？会给你的生活带来哪些不便？小词库里的词语可以帮助你表达。
Work in pairs, talking what will happen to you and what trouble are brought to you if any of the items above breaks down. The words in the Word Box may help you.

Word Box

臭(chōu smelly)、着急、难受、脏、热、冷、累、方便、害怕、危险(wēixiǎn dangerous)

※ 如果有不知道的词语，你可以查阅书后面的词汇表。
Look up new words in the Vocabulary Index at the end of the textbook when you encounter them.

3. 仔细看看下面的图片，然后从小词库里选择词语写在合适的图片下边。
Look at the following pictures, and then write the words from the Word Box under the appropriate pictures.

Word Box

坏、修、电脑、服务员、查、词典、转、洗衣机(xǐyījī washing machine)、打字(dǎzì to type)、服务台(fúwùtái reception desk)、烦(fán annoyed)

※ 除了这些词语，你还想到了什么词，也可以写在图片的旁边。
What other words come to you, apart from the words above? Write them next to the pictures.

※ 如果有不知道的词语，你可以问问老师或同学，也可以查阅书后面的词汇表。
Ask your teacher or look up new words in the Vocabulary Index at the end of the textbook when you encounter them.

4. 两人一组，和同伴一起说说图片的内容。
   Work in pairs and discuss the pictures.

   ☀ 同伴说的时候，你应该注意听。如果有听不懂的地方，一定要问问他(她)。
   Listen to your partner carefully and ask him/her about things you don't understand.

5. 请在图片旁边为每一幅图片写一两句话，简单叙述一下图片上的内容。
   Write one or two sentences next to each picture, simply narrating the picture story.

二、语言形式 Language Focus (约20分钟)

1. 和同伴一起看看下面的例句，复习可能补语。
   Work with your partner to review the potential complements.

● 可能补语主要表示是否允许某种结果或情况发生。它的主要形式是：动词+得/不+结果补语/趋向补语。例如：

The potential complement denotes whether a condition allows an action or a result to take place. Its main form is: 动词+得/不+ 结果补语/趋向补语. E.g.

老师写的字很大，我坐在后面也看得清楚。
我一点儿也不饿，这么多面条我吃不完。
这座山虽然很高，但是小王一定爬得上去。
路太远，走不回去，所以我们打算坐车回去。

2. 请你再看看这个图片故事，试着用可能补语写两个句子。
Look at the picture story again. Try to use the potential complement to write two sentences.

(1)

(2)

3. 和同伴一起看看下面的例句，复习"动词+得/不+了(liǎo)"构成的可能补语。
Work with your partner to review the following example sentences and the potential complement of "动词+得/不+了(liǎo)".

这个西瓜太大了，咱们俩吃不了。
今天没有电，看不了电视。
电冰箱坏了，用不了了。

4. 试着用一用"动词+得/不+了(liǎo)"的形式完成下面的句子。
Complete the following sentences with "动词+得/不+了(liǎo)".

(1) 今天的作业特别多，但是我感冒了，身体特别不舒服，所以

_____。

(2) 他的自行车坏了，_____

_____。

(3) 昨天晚上我们房间的电话坏了，_____，

所以我今天早上就来找你了。

●给老师的提示：这一题您可以采取先写后说的方式进行，并指导学生更好地使用可能补语使表达更准确。

写作任务 Writing Task

一、组织材料 Organizing Materials （约10分钟）

两人一组，和同伴一起按照图片故事的内容，回答下面的问题。
Work in pairs. Answer the following questions according to the picture story.

(1) 大卫今天打算干什么？

(2) 他的电脑出了什么问题？

(3) 他为什么不继续写信了？

(4) 他洗衣服的时候，洗衣机怎么了？

(5) 他今天洗衣服了吗？为什么？

(6) 今天大卫过得怎么样？为什么？

☀ 为了使你们的故事更合理，更有意思，有的部分需要你们发挥想象力，补充细节。
In order to make your story more realistic and interesting, use your imagination to add some details.

●给老师的提示：这一题您可以带着全班一起完成，尽量启发学生发挥想象力，为故事补充细节。

二、 动手写 Getting It Down （约20分钟）

请你按照上面6个问题的顺序，用20分钟写出这个图片故事。
According to the order of the 6 questions above, write a story about the pictures in 20 minutes.

☀ 不会写的字，可以先用拼音写。
If there are any characters that you cannot write, you may write them in Pinyin first.

写后修改　After Writing (约20分钟)

1. 与同伴交换所写的图片故事，看后回答问题。
   Exchange stories with your partner, and then answer the questions.

   (1) 他(她)写的句子你都能看懂吗？把看不懂的句子画出来，告诉他(她)。
   Do you understand everything your partner wrote? Mark the unclear sentences and ask him/her about them.

   (2) 比较一下你们俩写的图片故事。
   Compare your story with your partner's.

   ● 你们俩的图片故事中不一样的内容是：_____
   _____。

   (3) 和同伴讨论一下这些不一样的内容，看看哪一种更好。
   Discuss with your partner on the differences in content, and look at which is better.

   (4) 你们俩一起给故事写一个好的结尾。
   Work together on a good ending for the story.

(5) 你的同伴有没有写错字？有的话就告诉他(她)。

Are there any wrong characters? If there are, tell him/her.

(6) 如果有你不知道的词和不认识的字，就问问他(她)。

If there are any characters you do not recognize, ask him/her.

(7) 短文中的标点符号都写对了吗？帮他(她)检查一下。

Are there any punctuation marks used incorrectly? Help him/her check them.

> ☼ 互相检查，改正错误，遇到困难可以问老师。
> *Check what your partner wrote and correct the errors. Ask your teacher when you encounter difficulties.*

2. 改正自己短文中的错误，然后和其他小组交流一下。

Correct the errors in your paragraph and then discuss with other groups.

> ● 给老师的提示：您可以请几个学生朗读他们的文章，使同学们分享彼此的写作成果。您还可以从学生的文章中总结一些实用的结构写在黑板上，最后，做些简单、必要的讲解，作为本课的总结。

作业　Assignment

一、复习整理　Review

1. 整理本课所写过的句子和短文，把错句、错字改正后写在下边。

Review the sentences and paragraphs you wrote in this lesson, and correct the sentences and characters which were written incorrectly.

2. 整理本课所写过的句子和短文，将生词和新的结构找出来，写在下边，
   还可以用它们写几个新的句子，帮助自己记忆。

   Review the sentences and paragraphs you wrote in this lesson. Pick out the new words and structures and write them down. Make some new sentences with them to help you memorize them.

二、补充提高 Growing and Improving

1. 对你写的短文再进行一次补充和修改，然后抄写在作业本上交给老师批改。

   Revise the paragraph again and add the new content. Rewrite your paragraph and hand it in to your teacher.

2. 在生活中你最怕出现什么情况？写一段话说说原因。

   What are you afraid of most in your daily life? Write a paragraph to explain the reasons.

   ⊕ 要注意充分利用你在这一课学习的所有新词、新结构等，并尽量吸取其他同学文章中的成功之处。

   Make use of the new words, structures, etc. in this lesson, and try your best to absorb the strong points from what your classmates wrote.

8

热情的邻居

学习目标 Objective

学习描述在生活中遇到的问题及解决问题的经过
Learn to narrate the experience of encountering and
solving problems in your daily life

写前准备 Before Writing

一、热身活动 Warm-Up (约30分钟)

1. 仔细看看下面的图片，把你想到的词语写在对应的图片下边。
Look at the following pictures, and then write the words that come to you under the appropriate pictures.

◎ 不会写的词语，可以先用拼音写。
If there are any characters you cannot write, write them in *Pinyin* first.

2. 两人一组，和同伴一起说说，你觉得图片上的留学生遇到了什么问题？他们应该怎么办？小词库里的词语可以帮助你表达。

Work in pairs and discuss what trouble happens to the foreign student in the pictures and how he solves the problems. The words in the Word Box may help you.

Word Box

问、邻居、气、坏、求助(qiúzhù to ask for help)、路人 (lùrén passerby)、迷路(mílù to lose one's way)、修车铺 (xiūchēpù vehicle repairing stall)

❋ 如果有不知道的词语，你可以查阅书后面的词汇表。
Look up the new words in the Vocabulary Index at the end of the textbook when you encounter them.

3. 仔细看看下面的图片，然后从下面小词库里选择词语写在合适的图片下边。

Look at the following pictures, and then choose words from the Word Box and write them under the appropriate pictures.

Word Box

着急、钥匙、帮、面条、关心、打听、还(huán to give back)、感谢、借、推、缴费单(jiǎofèidān bill)、车棚(chēpéng shed)、嘱咐(zhǔfù to advise)

_____

_____

6

☀ 如果有不知道的词语，你可以问问老师或同学，也可以查阅书后面的词汇表。
Ask your teacher or look up new words in the Vocabulary Index at the end of the textbook when you encounter them.

4. 两人一组，和同伴一起说说图片的内容。
Work in pairs and discuss the pictures.

☀ 同伴说的时候，你应该注意听。如果有听不懂的地方，一定要问问他(她)。
Listen to your partner carefully and ask him/her about things you don't understand.

5. 读一读下面的句子，然后将句子分别抄写在合适的图片旁边。
Read the following sentences, and then write the appropriate sentences next to the pictures.

(1) 王大妈很关心大卫。知道大卫病了，她做了好吃的面条来看大卫。

(2) 中午，大卫去王大爷家还自行车，王大爷已经修好了他的自行车。王大爷还告诉大卫，以后有什么事都可以来找他。

(3) 大卫回家的时候，看到门上有一张煤气(méiqì gas)缴费单，他不知道应该怎么办，所以打电话问王大妈。

(4) 王大爷看到大卫着急的样子，就把自己的自行车借给了他。

(5) 大卫急急忙忙地来到车棚拿自行车，没想到他的车坏了，不能骑。如果不骑自行车去上课，他一定会迟到的。

(6) 大卫嘴里说着"谢谢！"，骑着王大爷的自行车去学校了。

二、 语言形式 Language Focus （约20分钟）

1. 和同伴一起看看下面的例句，然后每个人用不同的语言表达形式说一个新句子。
   Work with your partner to review the following example sentences, and then each says a new sentence using each structure.

   - "当……时(的时候)，……"表示时间。例如：
     "当……时(的时候)，……" indicates time. E.g.

     我很想帮妈妈做饭，可是当我回到家里的时候，妈妈已经把饭做好了。
     安妮今天起晚了，当她急急忙忙赶到车站时，同学们已经走了。

   - "不管……都……"表示在任何情况下，情况或结论都不会改变。例如：
     "不管……都……" indicates state or result won't change in any conditions. E.g.

     我告诉他，不管遇到什么样的困难都可以找老师商量。
     不管是中国学生还是留学生都不应该迟到。
     这部电影很受欢迎，不管男女老少都喜欢看。

2. 请你试着用"当……时（的时候），……"改写94页、95页热身活动第5题中的第1、3、4这3个句子。
   Try to use "当……时（的时候），……" to rewrite the 1st, 3rd and

4th sentences in the No.5 of the Warm-Up section on pages 94 and 95.

(1)

(3)

(4)

3. 请你试着用"不管……都……"改写94页热身活动第5题中的第2个句子。

Try to use "不管……都……" to rewrite the 2nd sentence in the No.5 of the Warm-Up section on page 94.

●给老师的提示：这一题您可以采取先写后说的方式进行，并指导学生更准确地表达。

写作任务 Writing Task

一、组织材料 Organizing Materials （约20分钟）

1. 阅读课文，并回答问题。
   Read the text and answer the questions.

热情的邻居

　　大卫刚刚租了一套房子，谁也不认识。王大爷和王大妈是他的邻居。

　　有一天早晨，大卫起晚了，急急忙忙(jíjímāngmāng hastily)来到楼下的车棚，要骑自行车去上课，没想到他的车坏了，不能骑。他看看表已经7点45分了，如果走着去学校，上课就要迟到了。王大爷看到了大卫很着急的样子，走过去对他说："你骑我的自行车去吧，别迟到了。"大卫说了一声"谢谢"就骑上车走了。

　　王大爷真是个热心(rèxīn warm-hearted)的人，还帮大卫修好了自行车。中午大卫去王大爷家还自行车的时候，王大爷还告诉大卫，以后不管遇到什么事情都可以来找他。

　　从那天以后，大卫和王大爷成了好朋友。他有了问题就打电话问王大爷或者王大妈。王大妈也非常关心大卫。大卫生病的时候，王大妈会给他做好吃的面条。

　　大卫非常高兴有这样的好邻居。

(1) 大卫的自行车怎么了？

(2) 大卫后来是怎么去上课的？

(3) 大卫为什么和王大爷成了朋友？

●给老师的提示：这一题您可以带着全班一起完成，尽量启发学生发挥想象力，为图片故事补充细节。

2. 两人一组，参考下面的问题，给你的同伴介绍一下你在中国的生活。
Work in pairs and introduce your life in China to your partner referring to the following questions.

(1) 你来中国以后遇到过什么问题？你是怎么解决的？

(2) 你认识你的邻居吗？你们互相帮助过吗？

(3) 你有中国朋友吗？你们是怎么认识的？

3. 在你刚才谈到的问题中选择一个，利用下面的问题整理一下思路。
Choose one topic from what you talked about. Use the following questions to gather your thoughts.

(1) 你遇到了什么问题？

(2) 什么时候遇到的这个问题？

(3) 遇到这个问题的时候，你想到了什么？

(4) 有没有人帮助你？

(5) 你是怎么解决这个问题的？

二、动手写 Getting It Down (约20分钟)

请你用20分钟写一段话，介绍一下你在中国遇到问题和解决问题的经过。
Write a paragraph in 20 minutes, to introduce troubles you have encountered in China and how you solved them.

☀ 不会写的字，可以先用拼音写。
If there are any characters that you cannot write, you may write them in *Pinyin* first.

写后修改 **After Writing** (约10分钟)

1. 与同伴交换所写的短文，看后回答问题。
Exchange paragraphs with your partner and then answer the following questions.

(1) 他(她)写的句子你都能看懂吗？把看不懂的句子画出来，告诉他(她)。
Do you understand everything your partner wrote? Mark the unclear sentences and ask him/her.

(2) 他(她)遇到了什么问题？
What trouble did he/she encounter?

(3) 他(她)的问题是怎么解决的？有人帮助他(她)吗？

how did he/she solve the trouble? It there anybody helping him/her out?

(4) 你的同伴有没有写错字？有的话就告诉他(她)。

Are there any wrong characters? If there are, tell him/her.

(5) 如果有你不知道的词和不认识的字，就问问他(她)。

If there are any characters you do not recognize, ask him/her.

(6) 短文中的标点符号都写对了吗？帮他(她)检查一下。

Are there any punctuation marks used incorrectly? Help him/her check them.

☀ 互相检查，改正错误，遇到困难可以问老师。

Check what your partner wrote and correct the errors. Ask your teacher when you encounter difficulties.

2. 改正自己短文中的错误，然后和其他小组交流一下。

Correct the errors in your notes and then discuss with other groups.

● 给老师的提示：您可以请几个学生朗读他们的文章，使同学们分享彼此的写作成果。您还可以从学生的文章中总结一些实用的结构写在黑板上，最后做些简单、必要的讲解，作为本课的总结。

作业 Assignment

一、复习整理 Review

1. 整理本课所写过的句子和短文，把错句、错字改正后写在下边。

Review the sentences and paragraphs you wrote in this lesson, and correct the sentences and characters which were written incorrectly.

2. 整理本课所写过的句子和短文，将生词和新的结构找出来，写在下边，还可以用它们写几个新的句子，帮助自己记忆。

Review the sentences and paragraphs you wrote in this lesson. Pick out the new words and structures and write them down. Make some new sentences with them to help you memorize them.

二、补充提高 Growing and Improving

1. 对你写的短文再进行一次补充和修改，然后抄写在作业本上交给老师批改。

   Revise the paragraph again and add the new content. Rewrite your paragraph and hand it in to your teacher.

2. 最近你有什么问题吗？写一段话说说你遇到的问题。

   Have you encountered any troubles recently? Write a paragraph to narrate the troubles.

   ◈ 要注意充分利用你在这一课学习的所有新词、新结构等，并尽量吸取其他同学文章中的成功之处。

   Make use of the new words, structures, etc. in this lesson, and try your best to absorb the strong points from what your classmates wrote.

难忘的生日

学习简单叙述过生日的经历

Learn to narrate the experience of celebrating a birthday

写前准备 Before Writing

一、热身活动 Warm-Up (约30分钟)

1. 你喜欢过生日吗? 为什么? 把你想到的词语写在下面。
   Do you like to celebrate birthdays? Why? Write down the words that come to you below.

   ◎ 写词语，不要写句子。
   Write words and phrases instead of sentences.

2. 两人一组，给同伴说一说你的看法。
   Work in pairs and share ideas about celebrating a birthday.

3. 仔细看看下面的图片，然后从小词库里选择词语写在合适的图片下边。
   Look at the following pictures, and then write the words from the Word Box under the appropriate pictures.

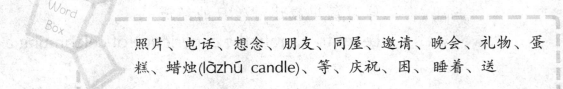

照片、电话、想念、朋友、同屋、邀请、晚会、礼物、蛋糕、蜡烛(làzhú candle)、等、庆祝、困、睡着、送

如果有不知道的词语，你可以问问老师或同学，也可以查阅书后面的词汇表。

Ask your teacher or look up new words in the Vocabulary Index at the end of the textbook when you encounter them.

_____

_____

妈妈
我很快乐!

祝你生日快乐!

_____

4. 两人一组，和同伴一起说说图片的内容。
   Work in pairs and discuss the pictures.

   ☀ 同伴说的时候，你应该注意听。如果有听不懂的地方，一定要问问他(她)。
   Listen to your partner carefully and ask him/her about things you don't understand.

5. 请在图片旁边为每一幅图片写一两句话，简单叙述一下图片的内容。
Write one or two sentences next to each picture, narrating the picture story.

> 不会写的字，可以先用拼音写。
> If there are any characters you cannot write, write them in Pinyin first.

● 给老师的提示：这一题您可以采取先写后说的方式进行。

二、语言形式 Language Focus (约20分钟)

1. 和同伴一起看看下面的例句，复习兼语句。
Work with your partner to review the example sentences and the pivotal sentences.

● 兼语句前一个动宾短语的宾语也是后一个主谓短语的主语。例如：
In a pivotal sentence the object of the first verb functions at the same time as the subject of the second verb. E.g.

他的话使我 +

我 十分生气 → 他的话使我十分生气。

2. 和同伴一起试着用下面句中的动词说几个兼语句。
Work in pairs and say several pivotal sentences with the verbs in the following sentences.

我想请你参加一个晚会。

老师让我们唱了一支歌。

他们要求我提前一小时到教室去。

同学们的帮助使我非常感动。

3. 你针对图3用兼语句写一个句子。
According to picture 3, write a pivotal sentence.

●给老师的提示：这一题您可以采取
先写后说的方式进行，并指导学生选
择更好的表达方式。

写作任务 Writing Task

一、组织材料 Organizing Materials （约20分钟）

1. 想一想你最难忘的一个生日，把你想到的最重要的词语或者句子写在下面。
   Think about a memorable birthday, and write down the most important
   words or sentences that come to you.

◎ 不会写的字，可以先用拼音写。
If there are any characters you cannot
write, write them in Pinyin first.

2. 两人一组，给同伴讲一讲你的那个难忘的生日，并说明让你难忘的主要原因。

Work in pairs and talk about that memorable birthday, especially explaining the main reasons why it is memorable.

3. 阅读安妮写的日记，并回答问题。

Read the diary Anne wrote and answer the questions.

安妮的日记(rìjì diary)

6月2日　星期三　晴

　　今天是我18岁的生日，也是我在中国过的第一个生日。早晨我就躺在床上看照片，那是去年过生日时照的。那天，爸爸和妈妈请我的朋友们到家里来，给我举行了一个生日晚会，大家还送给我很多礼物。可是今天……当时我特别想家。

　　中午一下课我就回宿舍了，我要等妈妈的电话。因为今天妈妈一定会给我打电话的。我坐在桌子旁边，等着妈妈的电话。电话响了，但不是妈妈，是同屋。她请我晚上参加一个晚会，我高兴地接受了邀请。

　　妈妈的电话一直没来，结果我困了，不知不觉(bù zhī bù jué unconscious)睡着了。当我醒来的时候，天已经黑了。我赶紧去教室参加晚会。推开教室的门，我看到桌子上有一个大蛋糕，蛋糕上有很多蜡烛。大家看到我来了，一起为我唱了生日歌，还送给我很多礼物。我非常感动，也非常高兴。

　　晚上，妈妈来电话的时候，我告诉妈妈，我今天很快乐。

(1) 今天安妮为什么特别想家？

(2) 去年她的生日是怎么过的？

(3) 为什么安妮一下课赶紧回宿舍？

(4) 她接到了谁的电话？有什么事儿？

(5) 晚上她来到教室里看到了什么？

(6) 安妮18岁的生日过得怎么样？为什么？

●给老师的提示：这一题您可以带着全班一起完成。并请您参考书后面的"汉语常用标点符号一览表"，提醒学生注意省略号的用法。

4. 利用下面的问题，整理一下你的思路.
Put your thoughts together according to the following questions.

(1) 你最希望怎样过生日？

(2) 过那个难忘的生日时你多少岁？

(3) 那天你快乐吗？为什么？

(4) 那天你都做了什么？谁和你在一起？

(5) 你喜欢这样过生日吗？

☺ 只写出重要的词语或句子就可以了，不用写得太多。
Just write the key words or sentences, and you don't need to write too much.

二、动手写 Getting It Down (约20分钟)

请你用20分钟写一段话，介绍一下你生日那天的事情。
In 20 minutes, write a paragraph to introduce the experience of that birthday.

☺ 你也可以模仿课文，用日记的形式写。
Follow the text to write it in the correct form of a diary.

1. 与同伴交换所写的短文，看后回答问题。
   Exchange paragraphs with your partner and then answer the following questions.

   (1) 你的同伴所写的生日是什么样的？请你选择。
      Which word best describes the birthday your partner wrote about?

      ☐ 快乐(kuàilè enjoyable)的一天
      ☐ 寂寞(jìmò lonely)的一天
      ☐ 幸福(xìngfú happy)的一天
      ☐ 伤心(shāngxīn heartbroken)的一天
      ☐ 无聊(wúliáo boring)的一天
      ☐ 紧张(jǐnzhāng nervous)的一天

   ⦿ 互相检查，改正错误，
   遇到困难可以问老师。
   *Check what your partner
   wrote and correct the errors.
   Ask your teacher when you
   encounter difficulties.*

   (2) 这是他(她)哪一年的生日？
      What year did he/she celebrate the birthday?

   (3) 他(她)的这个生日是在哪儿过的？
      Where did he/she celebrate the birthday?

   (4) 你觉得他(她)介绍得清楚吗？关于他(她)的生日你还想知道什么？
      Do you think his/her introduction is clear? What else do you want to know?

   (5) 你的同伴有没有写错字？有的话就告诉他(她)。
      Are there any wrong characters? If there are, tell him/her.

   (6) 如果有你不知道的词和不认识的字，就问问他(她)。
      If there are any characters you do not recognize, ask him/her.

   (7) 短文中的标点符号都写对了吗？帮他(她)检查一下。
      Are there any punctuation marks used incorrectly? Help him/her check them.

2. 改正自己短文中的错误，然后和其他小组交流一下。
Correct the errors in your paragraph and then discuss with other groups.

●给老师的提示：您请几个学生朗读他们的文章，使同学们分享彼此的写作成果。您还可以从学生的文章中总结一些实用的结构写在黑板上，最后做些简单、必要的讲解，作为本课的总结。

作 业 Assignment

一、复习整理 Review

1. 整理本课所写过的句子和短文，把错句、错字改正后写在下边。
Review the sentences and paragraphs you wrote in this lesson, and correct the sentences and characters which were written incorrectly.

2. 整理本课所写过的句子和短文，将生词和新的结构找出来，写在下边，还可以用它们写几个新的句子，帮助自己记忆。

Review the sentences and paragraphs you wrote in this lesson. Pick out the new words and structures and write them down. Make some new sentences with them to help you memorize them.

二、补充提高 Growing and Improving

1. 对你写的短文再进行一次补充和修改，然后抄写在作业本上交给老师批改。

Revise the paragraph again and add the new content. Rewrite your paragraph and hand it in to your teacher.

2. 写一篇短文，介绍一下对你来说最难忘的一天。

Write a paragraph to describe one of your most memorable days.

⊙ 要注意充分利用你在这一课学习的所有新词、新结构等，并尽量吸取其他同学文章中的成功之处。

Make use of the new words, structures, etc. in this lesson, and try your best to absorb the strong points from what your classmates wrote.

一件小事

Learn to narrate a matter

学习简单叙述一件事情
Learn to narrate a matter

写前准备 Before Writing

一、 热身活动 Warm-Up (约30分钟)

1. 仔细看看下面的图片，把你想到的词语写在对应的图片下边。
Look at the following pictures, and then write the words that come to you under the appropriate pictures.

_____

_____

_____

_____

_____

_____

2. 两人一组，看看你和同伴写的词语一样不一样，然后一起说说图片的内容。

   Work in pairs. Look at whether the words you wrote are the same as your partner's, and then talk about the pictures together.

● 给老师的提示：在做这一题之前，您可以请几组到黑板上写出他们准备的词语，并为他们补充一些。使学生在说的过程中有更多的词语可以使用。

◦ 同伴说的时候，你应该注意听。如果有不知道的词语，一定要问问他(她)。
Listen to your partner carefully and ask him/her about things you don't understand.

3. 请为每一幅图片写几句话，叙述一下这个留学生买西瓜的事情。

   Write several sentences for each picture and tell the story about the foreign student buying watermelons.

◦ 不会写的字，可以先用拼音写。
If there are any characters that you cannot write, you may write them in Pinyin first.

● 给老师的提示：这一题您可以采取先写后说的方式进行。

二、语言形式 Language Focus (约20分钟)

1. 和同伴一起看看下面的例句，然后每个人用不同的语言表达形式说一个新句子。
Work with your partner to review the following example sentences, and then each says a new sentence using each structure.

- "由于"表示原因。用在句子的前一部分，后一部分说明结果。例如：
"由于" indicates a cause, which is introduced in the first half of the sentence, while the second half denotes effects. E.g.

由于天气不好，今天早晨上班时，所有的人都带着雨伞。
由于爸爸妈妈都不同意我出国留学，我只好留在国内继续学习。

- "因此"用于表示结果或结论的句子或段落中。表示因果关系。有"因为……，所以……"的意思。前一分句也常用"由于"。例如：
"因此" is used in sentences or paragraphs to indicate results, or conclusions. It indicates a cause-effect relationship, having the meaning of "because ..., so ...". "由于" is also used in the first half of a sentence.

由于大家都喜欢这个活动，因此报名参加的人非常多。
如果没做好准备就去旅行，一定会发生很多问题。因此，出发前应该做好各方面的准备。

2. 针对图片3的内容写几句话，试着用一用"由于……，……"或者"……，因此……"。
Write several sentences according to picture 3. Try to use 由于……，……" or "……，因此……".

3. 和同伴一起看看下面的例句，复习状态补语。

Work with your partner, looking at the following example sentences and reviewing the manner of complements.

他高兴得流下了眼泪。

他高兴得跳起来了。

他累得连饭也不想吃了。

他累得一步也走不动了。

4. 请根据图1和图5的内容写两个句子，试着用一用状态补语。

Write two sentences according to pictures 1 and 5 respectively, using the manner of complements.

(1)

(2)

● 给老师的提示：这两题您可以采取先写后说的方式进行，并指导学生表达得更准确。

写作任务 Writing Task

一、组织材料 Organizing Materials （约20分钟）

1. 想一想你刚来中国的时候，有没有碰到过什么特别的事情？将你想到的重要词语写在下面。

What is something special that happened to you when you first came to China? Write down the key words that come to you below.

2. 三人一组，挑一件记得最清楚的事情给你的同伴讲一讲。
Work in a group of 3. Talk about what you remember most vividly to your partner.

◎ 听的人要注意边听边询问原因或结果。
The listener should ask about causes or effects while listening.

3. 阅读课文，并回答问题。
Read the text and answer the questions.

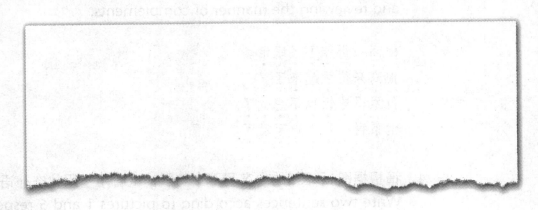

真不好意思

我刚到中国的时候，虽然只会说几句汉语，但是我很愿意说汉语。

有一次，我路过一个卖西瓜的小摊儿，看到有一个西瓜非常好，就随便问了一句："西瓜怎么卖？"老板说："五毛。"我一听非常高兴，心想：中国的东西真便宜，才五毛钱就能买到这么大的西瓜。所以我赶紧拿出五毛钱，指着那个又大又好的西瓜，对老板说："我要这个。"可是老板称了一下西瓜，然后对我说："六块二，给六块吧。"我吃惊(chījīng surprised)地看看老板，又看看我手里的五毛钱。这时老板对我说："不是五毛钱，是六块二。"我不明白为什么，因此非常生气，气得说不出话来。我觉得这个老板一定在骗我。过了一会儿，我对他说："你骗我吗？"老板好像明白了，他笑了笑说："好吧，你就给五毛钱吧！不过你回去以后要努力学习汉语！"结果，我只花了五毛钱就买了一个大西瓜。

　　我带着大西瓜回到宿舍，把这件事告诉了朋友们，朋友们听了都笑了。由于我的汉语水平太低，又不了解中国的情况，出了这样的事情，真是不好意思。从那天以后，我每天都努力地学习汉语。

(1) 大卫为什么要买一个大西瓜？

(2) 大卫听说是"六块钱"时为什么气得说不出话来？

(3) 老板最后为什么只要了五毛钱？

(4) 大卫为什么感到不好意思？

●给老师的提示：这一题您可以带着全班一起完成。并请您参考书后面的"汉语常用标点符号一览表"，提醒学生注意问号和感叹号的用法。

4. 利用下面的问题整理一下思路，想想怎样写出你想到的那件事。
Use the following questions to gather your thoughts. Think how to write about the matter that happened to you.

(1) 那是什么时候发生的事情？

(2) 你为什么到现在还没忘记这件事情？

(3) 为什么会发生这件事情？

(4) 事情的经过是怎样的？

(5) 事情的结果是怎样的？

●给老师的提示：这一题是帮助学生确定写作内容和写作顺序的，所以，您可以结合前面的课文，引导学生注意如何才能把事情叙述清楚；怎样交代前因后果更好。

二、动手写 Getting It Down (约20分钟)

请你用20分钟写一段话，讲一件发生在你生活中的一件小事。

In 20 minutes, write a paragraph to narrate something that happened in your life.

※ 不会写的字，可以先用拼音写。

If there are any characters that you cannot write, you may write them in Pinyin first.

写后修改 After Writing (约10分钟)

1. 与同伴交换所写的短文，看后回答问题。

Exchange paragraphs with your partner and then answer the following questions.

(1) 他(她)写的句子你都能看懂吗？把看不懂的句子画出来，告诉他(她)。

Do you understand everything your partner wrote? Mark the unclear sentences and ask him/her.

(2) 这件事情的经过他(她)写得清楚吗？如果有不清楚的地方，你可以问问他(她)。

Do you think his/her description is clear? If there is anything unclear, ask him/her about it.

(3) 这件事情发生的时间和地点，他(她)写清楚了吗？

Did he/she write the times and venues clearly?

(4) 你的同伴有没有写错字？有的话就告诉他(她)。

Are there any wrong characters? If there are, tell him/her.

(5) 如果有你不知道的词和不认识的字，就问问他(她)。

If there are any characters you do not recognize, ask him/her.

(6) 短文中的标点符号都写对了吗？帮他(她)检查一下。

Are there any punctuation marks used incorrectly? Help him/her check them.

☀ 互相检查，改正错误，遇到困难可以问老师。

Check what your partner wrote and correct the errors. Ask your teacher when you encounter difficulties

2. 改正自己短文中的错误，然后和其他小组交流一下。

Correct the errors in your paragraph and then discuss with other groups.

● 给老师的提示：您可以请几个学生朗读他们的文章，使同学们分享彼此的写作成果。您还可以从学生的文章中总结一些实用的结构写在黑板上，最后做些简单、必要的讲解，作为本课的总结。

作业 Assignment

一、复习整理 Review

1. 整理本课所写过的句子和短文，把错句、错字改正后写在下边。
   Review the sentences and paragraphs you wrote in this lesson, and correct the sentences and characters which were written incorrectly.

2. 整理本课所写过的句子和短文，将生词和新的结构找出来，写在下边，还可以用它们写几个新的句子，帮助自己记忆。
   Review the sentences and paragraphs you wrote in this lesson. Pick out the new words and structures and write them down. Make some new sentences with them to help you memorize them.

二、补充提高 Growing and Improving

1. 对你写的短文再进行一次补充和修改，然后抄写在作业本上交给老师批改。

   Revise the paragraph again and add the new content. Rewrite your paragraph and hand it in to your teacher.

2. 回忆一下你的童年，写一件童年时你最难忘的事情。

   Think about your childhood and write about one of your most memorable experiences.

   ☀ 要注意充分利用你在这一课学习的所有新词、新结构等，并尽量吸取其他同学文章中的成功之处。

   Make use of the new words, structures, etc. in this lesson, and try your best to absorb the strong points from what your classmates wrote.

复习（二）

一、单元自测 Self-Test

按自测问题选择或填写。
Choose or fill in the form according to the self-test questions.

自测问题 Self-Test Questions	试着选择或写出你的答案 Choose or Write the Answers
1. 你现在能说明一些生病时的症状和生病的原因了吗？ Can you describe some symptoms of illness and explain its causes?	A 能　B 还可以　C 不能
2. 请试着写出一些表示身体部位的词语。 Write some words relating to the parts the human body.	头、
3. 你能够简单地说明生活用品和设施的常见故障了吗？ Can you explain common malfunctions of daily articles and facilities?	A 能　B 还可以　C 不能
4. 请试着写出几种生活用品和设施的常见故障。 Write about several common malfunctions of daily articles and facilities.	电脑：　　　　电梯： 电话：　　　　空调： 洗衣机：
5. 你能简单介绍自己遇到的问题和解决问题的经过了吗？ Can you briefly describe a problem that happened to you and how you solved it?	A 能　B 还可以　C 不能
6. 你能简单地介绍自己过生日的经历了吗？ Can you write a paragraph describing one of your birthdays?	A 能　B 还可以　C 不能

7. 请写出一些在庆祝生日时常见的物品和庆祝方式。 Write the names of some items and activities used to celebrate birthdays.	物品：花 庆祝方式：和朋友一起吃饭
8. 你能够简单、清楚地写出一件在生活中遇到的小事了吗？ Can you clearly and briefly write about a matter you encountered in your life?	A 能　B 还可以　C 不能
9. 请试着写出几个表示原因和结果的词语。 Write words indicating causes and results.	

二、复习与扩展　Review and Extension

1. 请仔细看每一组图，A图都表示原因，B图都表示结果。请根据图的内容写一两个表示原因和结果的句子，并用上下列词语。

   Look at the groups of pictures A and B. Group A indicates causes and B results. Use the following words to write one or two sentences suggesting causes and results.

Word Box

因为……所以……、由于……、……因此……

(1) _____

遇到生词可以查词典，也可以问问老师。
Ask your teacher when you encounter new words.

(2) _____

(3) _____

(4) _____

A

B

(5) _____

2. 看图写句子。看看你能写出几个带"了"的句子。
   Look at the pictures and write sentences with "了".

(1) _____

_____

_____

_____

(2) 跟一个同伴交换课本，互相学习，互相检查，并修改自己写得不好的句子。

   Exchange textbooks with your partner. Learn and check want he/she wrote. Revise your own sentences.

3. 下面这组图画的都是一件事，图C是这件事的结果。图B和图C之间缺少了一些内容。两人一组，再看看图，讨论一下图B和图C之间少了什么内容。最后根据这组图片的内容写一段话。

The following group of pictures talks about a small matter, and Picture C is the result of the matter. Between Picture B and C there lack some important contents. Work in pairs. Look at the pictures again and discuss what happens between Picture B and C. Finally write a paragraph according to the pictures.

三、写作工作室 Writing Workshop

全班一起出一期主题为"留学故事"的班报，每个同学为这个班报写一段话，讲讲你留学的故事。

Each student writes a paragraph for an edition of class newspaper to be titled Study Abroad.

1. 请你从下面的题目中选择一个比较感兴趣的题目。

   Choose a topic you are comparatively interested in from the following:

   ☐ 第一次说汉语

   ☐ 第一次自己上街

   ☐ 第一次去饭馆

   ☐ 第一次生病

   ☐ 第一次认识中国朋友

   ☐ 在中国过的第一个节日

   ☐ 一次误会(a misunderstanding)

   ☐ 一件麻烦事

2. 从全班同学中选一名编辑，向每个同学征稿。(编辑可以了解一下谁想写什么话题，如何安排班报的内容。注意：同学们写的话题应当丰富多样，选择同一个话题的人不能太多。)

Select an editor to collect contributions from the entire class. (Get a sense of what topic each has chosen and how to arrange the content. Pay attention to the variety of topics students have chosen. Avoid having too many students choose the same topic.)

3. 3～4人一个小组，一起谈谈自己选择的话题。注意一下别人是怎么介绍的，并互相提一些问题，使你们的介绍更清楚、更丰富。

Work in a group of 3 – 4, discussing your topic. Pay attention to how the others describe the experience and ask questions to each other, in order to make your introduction more clear and content-rich.

4. 大家分头准备自己的初稿，写好后互相检查修改。

Each person prepares his/her own first draft. After finishing, check and revise each other's first draft.

5. 把修改过的稿子重新抄好，最好再贴上一张你自己的照片。

Make a copy of the revised draft and paste a relevant photo on the copy.

6. 编辑和大家一起把所有材料按你们喜欢的形式在几张大一些的纸上布置好，然后贴在教室的墙上。

As a group, work together with the editor to cut and paste all the materials onto a large piece of paper in a format you choose and then paste it onto the wall in your classroom.

住在这里真方便

11

学习目标 Objective

学习介绍学生公寓及各种服务项目

Learn to introduce the students' dormitory and service facilities

一、热身活动 Warm-Up （约30分钟）

1. 看看下面的词语，然后将词语与对应的图片划线连接起来。
   Look at the words below, and then match them with the related pictures.

小卖部	洗衣机	饭馆	咖啡馆	阅览室	健身房
xiǎomàibù	xǐyījī	fànguǎn	kāfēi guǎn	yuèlǎn shì	jiānshēn fáng
a small shop	washing machine	a restaurant	a coffee shop	a reading room	a gym

◈ 不知道的词语可以问问别人，也可以查阅书后面的词汇表。
You can ask your teacher or look up new words in the Vocabulary Index at the end of the textbook when you encounter them.

2. 你住的地方方便吗？为什么？两人一组，从下面的几个方面说一说。

Is the place where you live convenient? Why? Work in pairs and talk with your partner referring to the following aspects.

☐ 学习
☐ 生活
☐ 娱乐(yúlè to entertain)
☐ 休息
☐ 健身(jiānshēn to keep fit)

⊛ 如果上面的内容还不够，你们可以加上自己认为重要的内容。
You may add details about what you think is important.

3. 仔细看看下面的图片，然后从下面的小词库里选择词语写在合适的图片下边。

Look at the following pictures, and then write the words from the Word Box under the appropriate pictures.

Word Box

报纸、杂志、电影、聊天儿、食品、洗、衣服、见面、电子邮件(diànzǐ yóujiàn email)、打扫(dǎsǎo to clean)、日用品(rìyòngpǐn daily commodities)、上网(shàngwǎng to surf the Net)

_____

_____

_____

_____

_____

_____

_____

_____

6

※ 如果有不知道的词语，你可以问问老师或同学，也可以查阅书后面的词汇表。
You can ask your teacher or look up new words in the Vocabulary Index at the end of the textbook when you encounter them.

4. 两人一组，和同伴一起说说图片的内容。
Work in pairs and discuss the pictures.

※ 同伴说的时候，你应该注意听。如果有听不懂的地方，一定要问问他(她)。
Listen to your partner carefully and ask him/her about things you don't understand.

5. 读一读下面的句子，然后将句子分别抄写在合适的图片旁边。
Read the following sentences aloud. And then write them next to the appropriate pictures.

(1) 服务员每天都会打扫房间。如果你有什么问题，也可以找服务员。

(2) 在学生公寓的二楼，有一个图书阅览室。你不但可以在那儿看书、看报，也可以在那儿写作业。

(3) 每一层都有公用(gōngyōng public)的电冰箱和洗衣机。

(4) 附近有很多饭馆，学生公寓的旁边就有一个饭馆和一个咖啡馆。

(5) 学生宿舍里不但有电视、电话和空调，还能免费(miǎnfèi free of charge)上网，给朋友发电子邮件很方便。

(6) 在学生公寓的大厅(dàtīng hall)里有很多小桌子，还有一个小卖部。

二、语言形式 Language Focus (约20分钟)

1. 和同伴一起看看下面的例句，复习下面的关联词语。
   Work with your partner to review the following example sentences and the following conjunction words.

   ● "只要……就……"表示必要条件。例如：
     "只要……就……" indicates a prerequisite. E.g.

     只要你有问题，就可以找服务员帮忙。
     只要你的衣服脏了，就可以拿到洗衣房去洗。
     只要是我们学校的留学生，就可以免费使用宿舍楼里的电冰箱。

   ● "只有……才……"表示唯一的条件。例如：
     "只有……才……" indicates a unique condition.

     只有需要买大东西的时候，我们才去学校外边。
     只有刚来的新同学才去小卖部买东西。

2. 请试着用"只要……就……"或者"只有……才……"回答下面的问题。
   Try to use "只要……就……" and "只有……才……" to answer the following questions.

   (1) 在家的时候，你的脏衣服都是自己洗吗？

   _____

   (2) 现在你常给朋友发电子邮件吗？你在哪儿发？

   _____

(3) 你每天都运动吗？一般什么时候运动？

_____

(4) 你经常去小卖部买东西吗？一般买什么东西？

_____

☀ 你应该注意这两组关联词语的区别。
Pay attention to the differences between the two conjunction phrases in usage.

3. 和同伴一起看看下面的例句，复习一下感叹句。
Work with your partner to read the following example sentences, and then review the exclamatives.

● 感叹句是直接表达感情的句子，句末一般用感叹号。例如：
An exclamative sentence is to directly express emotion. An exclamation mark is used at the end of the sentence.

今天我太高兴了！
这里的风景美极了！

4. 请你再看看图1到图6，试着写两个感叹句。
Look at the pictures 1 – 6 again and try to write two exclamatives.

(1)

(2)

●给老师的提示：这两题您可以采取先写后说的方式进行，并指导学生表达得更准确。

写作任务 Writing Task

一、组织材料 Organizing Materials （约20分钟）

1. 阅读课文。
Read the text.

住在这里真方便

　　我们学校的学生公寓一共有12层。一楼是大厅，二楼是阅览室，从三楼到十二楼都是学生宿舍。

　　这座楼的每间宿舍都可以住两个人，房间里有卫生间，也有电视、电话和空调，只要你有电脑，在房间里就可以上网，发电子邮件很方便。学生公寓的每一层都有公用的洗衣机和电冰箱。每两层还有一个服务员，早晨学生去上课以后，她们就会把房间打扫得干干净净。平时他们也会热情地帮助有困难的学生解决问题。

　　在这座大楼的二楼是学生阅览室，学生们可以在那儿读书、看报、写作业；在一楼还有一个小卖部，学生们在小卖部就可以买日用品和小食品(shípǐn snack)。一楼大厅里摆着很多桌椅，你可以和朋友们坐在那儿聊聊天、下下棋；如果你觉得饿了想吃点东西，公寓楼的附近就有饭馆和咖啡馆。

　　住在这个学生公寓可真方便啊！

●给老师的提示：这一题您可以带着全班一起完成。并提醒学生注意感叹句的用法。

2. 两人一组，先和同伴一起简单填写下面的表格，然后讨论一下课文是怎样介绍学生公寓的。
Work in pairs. Fill in the table together and then discuss how the text introduces the students' dormitory.

问　题	主要内容
学生公寓每一层都有什么？	
学生公寓的每一个房间里都有什么？	
学生公寓还有什么服务项目？	
你们觉得这个学生公寓怎么样？	

◈ 不要写太多，只写出重要的词语或句子就可以。
You don't need to write too much. Just note down the key words or sentences.

● 给老师的提示：学生完成这一题后，您可以请几个同学说一说他们的看法，并提醒学生注意应该有条理地介绍一个地方。

3. 两人一组，和同伴一起按照下面的问题谈谈你们自己的学生公寓。
Work in pairs. Talk about your dormitory referring to the following questions.

(1) 你们的学生公寓有几层？大约可以住多少位学生？

(2) 你们的房间里和每一层楼里都有什么？没有什么？

(3) 你们的学生公寓里有小卖部、健身房和阅览室吗？

(4) 有吃饭或者与朋友们见面的地方吗？

(5) 住在这那方便不方便？为什么？

◈ 无论你喜欢还是不喜欢你们的学生公寓，都应该注意说出原因。
No matter whether you like your dormitory or not, give the reasons why.

● 给老师的提示：这一题您可以带着全班一起完成，尽量启发学生收集材料，确定写作内容和顺序。

◈ 你也可以介绍一个你以前住过的宾馆或饭店。
Introduce a hotel that you have stayed in before.

请你参考课文的写法，用20分钟写一段话，介绍一下你们的学生公寓或者你喜欢的宾馆和饭店。

Follow the example text and write a paragraph in 20 minutes describing your dormitory or a hotel you like.

写后修改 After Writing (约10分钟)

1. 与同伴交换所写的短文，看后回答问题。

   Exchange paragraphs with your partner and then answer the following questions.

   (1) 他(她)写的句子你都能看懂吗？把看不懂的句子画出来，告诉他

(她)。

Do you understand everything your partner wrote? Mark the unclear sentences and ask him/her.

(2) 比较一下你们俩写的短文，看看你们俩住的公寓有什么不一样。

Compare your paragraph with your partner's and look at the differences in descriptions of the two dormitories.

(3) 和同伴讨论一下那些不一样的内容，看看怎么介绍更好。

Discuss with your partner on the differences of contents, and see which is better.

(4) 看看你们俩的介绍顺序一样不一样？你的同伴先介绍了什么？

Are the orders of descriptions are the same? What did your partner describe first?

(5) 你的同伴有没有写错字？有的话就告诉他(她)。

Are there any wrong characters? If there are, tell him/her.

(6) 如果有你不知道的词和不认识的字，就问问他(她)。

If there are any characters you do not recognize, ask him/her.

(7) 有时间的话，帮同伴检查一下标点符号用对了没有。

If time permits, help your partner check the punctuation marks.

◎ 互相检查，改正错误，遇到困难可以问老师。
Check what your partner wrote and correct the errors. Ask your teacher when you encounter difficulties.

2. 改正自己短文中的错误，然后和其他小组交流一下。

Correct the errors in your paragraph and then discuss with other groups.

●给老师的提示：您可以请几个学生朗读他们的文章，使同学们分享彼此的写作成果。您还可以从学生的文章中总结一些实用的结构写在黑板上，最后做些简单、必要的讲解，作为本课的总结。

作业　Assignment

一、复习整理 Review

1. 整理本课所写过的句子和短文，把错句、错字改正后写在下边。
Review the sentences and paragraphs you wrote in this lesson, and correct the sentences and characters which were written incorrectly.

2. 整理本课所写过的句子和短文，将生词和新的结构找出来，写在下边，还可以用它们写几个新的句子，帮助自己记忆。
Review the sentences and paragraphs you wrote in this lesson. Pick out the new words and structures and write them down. Make some new sentences with them to help you memorize them.

二、 补充提高 Growing and Improving

1. 对你写的短文再进行一次补充和修改，然后抄写在作业本上交给老师批改。

   Revise the paragraph again and add the new content. Rewrite your paragraph and hand it in to your teacher.

2. 写一篇短文，介绍一下你的房间。

   Write a paragraph to describe your room.

   ❋ 要注意充分利用你在这一课学习的所有新词、新结构等，并尽量吸取其他同学文章中的成功之处。

   Make use of the new words, structures, etc. in this lesson, and try your best to absorb the strong points from what your classmates wrote.

学习目标 Objective

学习简单介绍一个地方

Learn to describe a place

写前准备 Before Writing

一、热身活动 Warm-Up (约30分钟)

1. 看看下面的词语，然后将词语与对应的图片画线连接起来。
   Look at the following words and then match them with the appropriate pictures.

花	树	湖	山	长椅	绿草地
huā	shù	hú	shān	chángyǐ	lǜ(cǎo)dì
flower	tree	lake	hill	bench	lawn

☀ 不知道的词语可以问问别人，也可以查阅书后面的词汇表。
Ask your teacher or look up new words in the Vocabulary Index at the end of the textbook when you encounter them.

2. 两人一组，说说你们学校的校园是什么样的？校园里都有什么？
   Work in pairs talking how your school campus looks and what is in it.

3. 仔细看看下面的图片，然后从小词库里选择词语写在合适的图片下边。
   Look at the following pictures, and then write the words from the Word Box under the appropriate pictures.

Word Box

漂亮、照相、小路、前面、旁边、对面、门口、周围、雕塑(diāosù sculpture)、网球(wǎngqiú tennis)、树林(shùlín grove)、盆(pén basin)

☀ 如果有不知道的词语，你可以问问老师或同学，也可以查阅书后面的词汇表。
You can ask your teacher or look up the new words in the Vocabulary Index at the end of the textbook when you encounter them.

_____

_____

_____

_____

4. 两人一组，和同伴一起说说图片的内容。
   Work in pairs and discuss the pictures.

   ○ 同伴说的时候，你应该注意听。如果有听不懂的地方，一定要问问他(她)。
   Listen to your partner carefully and ask him/her about things you don't understand.

5. 请在图片旁边为每一幅图片写一两句话，简单叙述一下图片上的内容。
   Write one or two sentences next to each picture, describing the picture.

   ● 给老师的提示：这一题您可以采取先写后说的方式进行。

   ○ 不会写的字，可以先用拼音写。
   If there are any characters that you cannot write, you may write them in *Pinyin* first.

二、语言形式 Language Focus (约20分钟)

1. 和同伴一起看看下面的例句，复习下面的关联词语。
   Work with your partner to read the following example sentences, and then review the following conjunction words.

   ● "不但……而且……" 表示递进关系。后一分句比前一分句的意思更进了一层。例如：

   "不但……而且……" is used to indicate a further development in meaning in the second clause from what is stated in the first one. E.g.

   这个公园不但很大，而且还很漂亮。
   这里不但有中国学生，而且还有很多外国留学生。
   不但操场周围有很多树，而且宿舍楼的前面也有很多树。

   ● "即使……也……" 表示假设的让步关系。"即使" 引出假设的情况，后面表示结果不受这种情况的影响。例如：

   "即使……也……" is used to indicate a concessive relationship. "即使" introduces a hypothesis, and the second half of the sentence suggests that the result will not be influenced by the hypothesis.

   即使是在天气最热的夏季，我们学校里边也不热。
   即使再忙，晚饭后我也要到校园里转一转。

2. 请试着用"不但……而且……"或者"即使……也……"回答下列问题。
   Try to use "不但……而且……" or "即使……也……" to answer the following questions.

   (1) 图1上的学校大门口都有什么？

   _____

   (2) 如果人们从图2上的小路走过的时候，都可以看到什么？

   _____

   (3) 看看图3，什么人可以去这个图书馆看书和学习？

   _____

   (4) 图5上的礼堂好找吗？

   _____

3. 和同伴一起看看下面的例句，复习存现句。
   Work with your partner to read the following example sentences, and then review the existence-emergence sentences.

   - 存现句表示某个处所存在着某一事物，或某个处所有某种事物出现或消失。例如：
     The existence-emergence sentence indicates the existence, emergence and disappearance of something in some place.

     我家的门前种了几棵树，还摆着一些花。
     小院子里非常安静，每一间房子的窗户上都亮着灯。
     路的左边有一个商店，路的右边是一个咖啡馆。

4. 试着写3个存现句，介绍你们学校里你最喜欢的一个地方。
   Try to write three existence-emergence sentences, describing one of your favorite places on campus.

   (1)

   (2)

   (3)

●给老师的提示：
这两题您可以采取先写后说的方式进行，并指导学生表达得更准确。

写作任务 Writing Task

一、组织材料 Organizing Materials （约20分钟）

1. 阅读课文，并从课文中找出3个存现句。
   Read the text and identify three existence-emergence sentences in the text.

丽的校园

　　大卫很喜欢他们的校园，每天吃完晚饭，他都会在校园里散步。

　　学校有三个大门，东门、西门和北门。西门和北门比较小，门口也不太漂亮，但是东门很大，也很漂亮。东门的门口有很多花，一进门就能看到一些树，还有一块漂亮的大石头，上边写着"好好学习，天天向上"。很多学生都喜欢在这儿照相。

　　网球场的旁边有一片小树林，是学校里树最多的地方。校园里最大的绿地在图书馆的前面，那儿的草总是绿绿的，中间还有一个好看的雕塑。校园里最热闹的地方是礼堂，那里经常举行各种活动。礼堂在学校的中间，从每一条路都能走到那儿，所以即使你不知道礼堂在哪儿，也很容易找到。留学生公寓在学校的东边，离东门很近，周围不但有很多树，还有花和草地。在那儿，你一定能看见很多留学生正在和中国学生一起学习。

　　大卫最喜欢的是教学楼(jiāoxué lóu teaching building)后面那条小路，路的两边都是树，树下还有很多长椅，又漂亮又安静。这个地方不但大卫喜欢，而且很多老师和同学都喜欢，因为大家都觉得这是一个学习和休息的好地方。

●给老师的提示：这一题您可以带着全班一起完成，并应该提醒学生注意存现句的用法。

2. 两人一组，先和同伴一起简单填写下面的表格，然后讨论一下课文是怎样介绍校园的。
   Work in pairs to fill in the following table, and then discuss how the text describes the campus.

问　题	主　要　内　容
学校有几个大门？ 哪个最漂亮？	
什么地方树最多？ 什么地方草最绿？	
什么地方最热闹？ 为什么？	
留学生住在哪儿？	
大卫最喜欢哪儿？	

✿ 不要写太多，只写出重要的词语或句子就可以。

You don't need to write too much. Write key words or sentences.

3. 两人一组，给同伴介绍一下你们学校的校园。重点说说下面几个地方。
Work in pairs. Introduce your campus to your partner, and focus on the following places.

☐ 大门口 (dà ménkǒu school gate)
☐ 图书馆 (túshūguǎn library)
☐ 操场 (cāochǎng sports field)
☐ 礼堂 (lǐtáng auditorium)
☐ 学生宿舍 (xuéshēng sùsè   students' dormitory)

●给老师的提示：这一题您可以带着全班一起完成，尽量启发学生抓住重点和特点介绍。

✿ 如果上面的内容还不够，你们可以加上自己认为重要的内容。

You may add details that you think are important if the information provided is not enough.

二、动手写 Getting It Down (约20分钟)

请你用20分钟写一段话，介绍一下你们的校园。
In 20 minutes write a paragraph describing your campus.

写后修改 After Writing (约10分钟)

1. 与同伴交换所写的短文，看后回答问题。
   Exchange paragraphs with your partner, and then answer the questions.

   (1) 他(她)写的句子你都能看懂吗？把看不懂的句子画出来，告诉他(她)。
   Do you understand everything your partner has written? Mark the unclear sentences and ask him/her.

   (2) 你的同伴介绍了学校的哪些地方？
   Which places did your partner describe?

(3) 比较一下你们介绍的学校校园。
Compare your paragraph with your partner's.

● 你们俩介绍的不一样的地方是：＿＿＿＿＿＿＿＿

＿＿＿＿＿＿＿＿＿＿＿＿＿＿＿＿＿＿＿＿＿＿

(4) 你和同伴讨论一下你们介绍的不一样的地方，看看怎么介绍更好。
Discuss with your partner on the differences of the content, and look at which is better.

(5) 你的同伴有没有写错字？有的话就告诉他(她)。
Are there any wrong characters? If there are, tell him/her.

(6) 如果有你不知道的词和不认识的字，就问问他(她)。
If there are any characters you do not recognize, ask him/her.

(7) 有时间的话，帮同伴检查一下标点符号用对了没有。
If time permits, help your partner check the punctuation marks.

❀ 互相检查，改正错误，遇到困难可以问老师。
Check what your partner wrote and correct the errors. Ask your teacher when you encounter difficulties.

2. 改正自己短文中的错误，然后和其他小组交流一下。
Correct the errors in your notes and then discuss with other groups.

● 给老师的提示：您可以请几个学生朗读他们的文章，使同学们分享彼此的写作成果。您还可以从学生的文章中总结一些实用的结构写在黑板上，最后做些简单、必要的讲解，作为本课的总结。

作业 Assignment

一、复习整理 Review

1. 整理本课所写过的句子和短文，把错句、错字改正后写在下边。

   Review the sentences and paragraphs you wrote in this lesson, and correct the sentences and characters which were written incorrectly.

2. 整理本课所写过的句子和短文，将生词和新的结构找出来，写在下边，还可以用它们写几个新的句子，帮助自己记忆。

   Review the sentences and paragraphs you wrote in this lesson. Pick out the new words and structures and write them down. Make some new sentences with them to help you memorize them.

二、补充提高 Growing and Improving

1. 对你写的短文再进行一次补充和修改，然后抄写在作业本上交给老师批改。
    Revise the paragraph again and add the new content. Rewrite your paragraph and hand it in to your teacher.

2. 写一篇短文，介绍一下你的中学或小学的校园。
    Write a paragraph to introduce the campus of your middle school or primary school.

要注意充分利用你在这一课学习的所有新词、新结构等，并尽量吸取其他同学文章中的成功之处。
Make use of the new words, structures, etc. in this lesson, and try your best to absorb the strong points from what your classmate wrote.

我们的汉语课

学习说明主要课程的种类及学习情况

Learn to explain key courses and your studies

写前准备 Before Writing

一、热身活动 Warm-Up （约30分钟）

1. 仔细看看下面的图片，然后从小词库里选择词语写在合适的图片下边。
   Look at the following pictures, and then write the words from the
   Word Box under the appropriate pictures.

表演、戴、电视、辅导、互相、口语、阅读、听力、语法、写作课本、练习、报纸、笔记、本子、表达、服务员、字、问题、耳机(ěrjī earphone)、图片(túpiàn picture)

※ 如果有不知道的词语，你可以问问老师或同学，也可以查阅书后面的词汇表。
Ask your teacher or look up the new words in the Vocabulary Index at the end of the textbook when you encounter them.

2. 两人一组，先看看你们写在图片下边的词语一样不一样，然后一起说说图片的内容。

Work in pairs. Look at whether the words you wrote under the pictures are the same as your partner's? Then discuss the pictures.

❋ 要尽量使用你写在图片下边的词语。

Try to use the words you wrote under the pictures.

3. 请根据图片内容回答下面的问题。
   Answer the following questions according to the pictures.

   (1) 安娜他们班都上什么课？

   (2) 上课的时候他们做什么？

   (3) 下课以后安娜怎样学习汉语？

   ●给老师的提示：这一题您可以带着全班学生一起完成。

4. 请你在图片旁边为每一幅图片写几句话，简单说明一下图片上的情况。
   Write several sentences next to each picture, describing the picture.

   ●给老师的提示：学生写完以后，您可以请几个学生读一读他们写的句子，以达到互相交流的目的。

二、 语言形式 Language Focus (约20分钟)

1. 和同伴一起看看下面的例句，并试着说几个新句子。
   Work with your partner to review the following example sentences, and then each says several sentences using each structure.

   ● "有的"是指人或事物中的一部分，常常两个或两个以上连用，如"有的……，有的……"。例如：
   "有的" indicates a part of some things or some persons. Two or more "有的" are often used together. For example: "有的……，有的……". E.g.

   有的人喜欢热闹，有的人喜欢安静。
   我有的时候在教室学习，有的时候在宿舍学习。
   这些字有的我认识，有的我不认识。

● "或者"表示选择，常常两个或两个以上连用。如"或者……或者……"。例如：

"或者" means "or" and it is often used in series of two or more together.

明天的会很重要，一定要去一个人。或者你去，或者我去。
每天下午我都要学习两个小时汉语，或者在宿舍写作业，或者和中国朋友聊天儿。

● "一天比一天……"表示事情在随着时间的变化而变化，意思和"越来越……"差不多。例如：

"一天比一天……" indicates changes with time. The meaning is almost the same as "越来越……".

他的身体一天比一天好，再过两天就能出院了。
到了11月天气会一天比一天冷，不穿棉衣怎么行呢？

2. 请试着用"或者……，或者……"、"有的……，有的……"或者"一天比一天"回答下面的问题。
Try to use "或者……，或者……"，"有的……，有的……", or "一天比一天" to answer the following questions.

(1) 如果你一个月都不说汉语，你的汉语水平会怎么样？

_____

(2) 你们在口语课上一般都做什么？

_____

(3) 下课以后你怎样学习汉语？

_____

(4) 星期天你一般都做什么？

_____

●给老师的提示：这两题您可以采取先写后说的方式进行，并指导学生表达得更准确。

162

写作任务 Writing Task

一、组织材料 Organizing Materials （约20分钟）

1. 阅读课文。
   Read the text.

安娜学汉语

　　安娜是为了学汉语来中国的。刚来的时候，她的汉语不太好，但是她每天都认真上课，下课以后还看电视、找中国人练习口语。五个多月过去了，安娜会说的汉语一天比一天多，现在安娜已经能跟中国人聊天儿了。

　　这个学期，安娜他们班有语法课、口语课、听力课、阅读课和写作课。有的学生喜欢上听力课，有的学生喜欢上阅读课。安娜最喜欢上语法课和口语课。语法老师总是先给他们看一张图片，用图片教他们学词语，说句子，然后才学习教材上的课文，这样很容易记住那些生词和语法。口语老师会带着他们用汉语完成很多任务(rènwù task)，或者让他们表演，或者让他们讨论，有的时候还带他们出去参观和调查，让他们有机会和中国人聊天儿。

　　上个学期(xuéqī semester)，安娜特别怕上阅读课和写作课，因为她不会写汉字，上课的时候很紧张。现在她认识的汉字越来越多，也越来越喜欢上阅读课和写作课了。昨天阅读老师带着他们读了一篇报纸上的文章，写作老师还让他们写了《快乐的一天》。

　　安娜觉得，现在她的每一天都很快乐！

2. 两人一组，和同伴一起回答下面的问题。
   Work in pairs and answer the following questions.

   (1) 为什么安娜说汉语说得一天比一天好？

(2) 安娜喜欢上什么课？为什么？

(3) 以前安娜为什么怕上阅读课和写作课？现在怎么样？

(4) 安娜的留学生活怎么样？

●给老师的提示：这一题您也可以
带着全班一起完成，尽量启发学生
注意课文每一段的主要内容。

3. 你们班都上什么课？上课的时候，你们一般做什么？请简单填写下面的表格。
What courses do you attend? What do you usually do in class? Fill in the following table.

你们班上的课	你们上课时做的事

4. 两人一组，和同伴一起说说你们上课的情况。
Work in pairs talking about your class.

☀ 同伴说的时候，你应该注意听，如果
有听不懂的地方，一定要问问他(她)。
*Listen to your partner carefully and ask him/
her about things you don't understand.*

●给老师的提示：学生做完这一题
以后，您可以请几个人说一说。

二、动手写 Getting It Down （约20分钟）

请你按照下面这些问题的顺序，用20分钟写一段话，介绍一下你们班的汉语课和你自己的学习汉语的情况。

According to the order of the following questions, write a paragraph in 20 minutes to introduce your Chinese class and your Chinese study.

(1) 你现在在哪儿学汉语？

(2) 你们都上什么课？

(3) 上课的时候你们一般做什么？

(4) 你最喜欢上什么课？为什么？

(5) 下课以后，你怎样学汉语？

(6) 你觉得什么样的学习方法比较好？

※ 你并不需要回答问题，你应该按照问题的内容和顺序组织一段话。

You don't need to answer the following questions. Organize a paragraph according to the content and order.

写后修改　After Writing

1. 与同伴交换所写的短文，看后回答问题。
   Exchange paragraphs with your partner and then answer the following questions.

   (1) 他(她)写的句子你都能看懂吗？把看不懂的句子画出来，告诉他(她)。
   Do you understand everything your partner wrote? Mark the unclear sentences and ask him/her.

   (2) 关于你们班的课，你们俩的介绍有什么不一样吗？
   As to your course, is your description the same as your partner's?

   (3) 关于学习方法，你们俩的看法一样吗？
   Do you have the same view on learning methodologies?

   (4) 和同伴讨论一下什么样的学习方法比较好。
   Discuss with your partner on which studying methods are better.

   (5) 你的同伴有没有写错字？有的话就告诉他(她)。
   Are there any wrong characters? If there are, tell him/her.

   (6) 如果有你不知道的词和不认识的字，就问问他(她)。
   If there are any characters you do not recognize, ask him/her.

   (7) 有时间的话，帮同伴检查一下标点符号用对了没有。
   If time permits, help your partner check the punctuation marks.

   ❋ 互相检查，改正错误，遇到困难可以问老师。
   Check what your partner wrote and correct the errors. Ask your teacher when you encounter difficulties.

2. 改正自己短文中的错误，然后和其他小组交流一下。
Correct the errors in your paragraph and then discuss with other groups.

●给老师的提示：您可以请几个学生朗读他
们的文章，使同学们分享彼此的写作成果。
您还可以从学生的文章中总结一些实用的结
构写在黑板上，最后做些简单、必要的讲
解，作为本课的总结。

作业 Assignment

一、复习整理 Review

1. 整理本课所写过的句子和短文，把错句、错字改正后写在下边。
Review the sentences and paragraphs you wrote in this lesson, and correct the sentences and characters which were written incorrectly.

2. 整理本课所写过的句子和短文，将生词和新的结构找出来，写在下边，还可以用它们写几个新的句子，帮助自己记忆。

Review the sentences and paragraphs you wrote in this lesson. Pick out the new words and structures and write them down. Make some new sentences with them to help you memorize them.

二、补充提高 Growing and Improving

1. 对你写的短文再进行一次补充和修改，然后抄写在作业本上交给老师批改。

Revise the paragraph again and add the new content. Rewrite your paragraph and hand it in to your teacher.

2. 回忆一下你上中学时的情况，写一段话介绍一下那时的学习和生活。

Recall a time when you were in middle school and write a paragraph to describe your studies and life at that time.

> ◎ 要注意充分利用你在这一课学习的所有新词、新结构等，并尽量吸取其他同学文章中的成功之处。
>
> *Make use of the new words, structures, etc. in this lesson, and try your best to absorb the strong points from what your classmates wrote.*

我的假期计划

学习目标 Objective

学习简单说明计划或打算

Learn to explain your plans

写前准备 Before Writing

一、热身活动 Warm-Up (约30分钟)

1. 仔细看看下面的图片，把你想到的词语写在对应的图片下边。
Look at the following pictures carefully and write the words that come to you under the pictures.

假期打算干什么？

安娜

_____

_____

乔丹

_____

_____

幸子

_____

_____

大卫

金大成

一郎

2. 两人一组，看看你和同伴写的词语一样不一样，然后一起说说图片的内容。

Work in pairs. Look at whether the words you wrote under the pictures are the same as your partner's. Then discuss the pictures.

※ 同伴说的时候，你应该注意听。如果有不知道的词语，一定要问问他(她)。

Listen to your partner carefully and ask him/her about things you don't understand.

3. 请在图片旁边为每一幅图片写几句话，简单介绍一下那个同学放假时的打算。

   Write several sentences next to each picture to explain your classmate's plans for vacation.

   ◌ 不会写的字，可以先用拼音写。
   If there are any characters that you cannot write, you may write them in Pinyin first.

   ● 给老师的提示：这一题您可以采取先写后说的方式进行。

4. 放假以后你最想做的两件事情是什么？在表格中简单写出原因。

   Which two things do you want to do most during vocation? Fill in the table giving the reasons.

放假以后你最想做的事情	主 要 原 因
(1)	
(2)	

二、语言形式 Language Focus (约20分钟)

1. 和同伴一起看看下面的例句，复习连动句。

   Work with your partner to see the following example sentences, and then review the sentences with serial verb phrases.

   ● 后一个动作发生时，前一个动作已经结束。例如：
   The former action has ended when the latter action happens. E.g.

   他吃过晚饭散步去了。
   我们听完大卫讲的故事都笑了。

   ● 后一个动作是前一个动作的目的。例如：
   The latter action is the purpose of the former action. E.g.

我们去商店买东西。
安娜来中国学汉语。

● 前一个动作是后一个动作的方式、手段或工具。例如：
The former action is the means or method of the latter action. E.g.

中国人用筷子吃饭。
明天我坐火车去上海。

2. 请你再看看图1到图6，试着根据图片内容写3个连动句。
Look at pictures 1–6. Try to write three sentences with serial verb phrases according to the pictures.

(1)

(2)

(3)

3. 和同伴一起看看下面的例句，并试着说几个新句子。
Work with your partner to review the following example sentences, and then each says several sentences using each structure.

● "要么……要么……"表示在所说的两种情况中加以选择。例如：
"要么……要么……" indicates a choice between two conditions provided. E.g.

今天要么去逛商店，要么去看电影，你决定吧。
这一次要放10天假，我要么回国看看爸爸和妈妈，要么就去云南旅游。
你如果遇到不认识的字，要么问老师，要么查词典。

4. 请你利用172页热身活动第4题表格中的内容写两句话，试着用一用 "要么……要么……"。
Use the content in the No. 4 of the Warm-Up section on page 172 to write two sentences with "要么……要么……".

●给老师的提示：这两题您可以采取先写后说的方式进行，并指导学生表达得更准确。

写作任务　Writing Task

一、组织材料　Organizing Materials （约20分钟）

1. 阅读课文。
   Read the text.

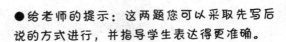

他们假期打算做什么

　　快要放假了，同学们都在考虑自己放假以后干什么。

　　有很多同学要参加汉语水平考试，所以放假以后他们要努力学习。金大成就打算报名参加一个HSK的辅导班。还有的同学假期要跟辅导老师继续学习汉语。

　　除了打算学习的同学以外，有一些同学计划去旅游。大卫就是个旅游迷(mí fan)，这一次他打算一个人去南方(nánfāng southern part of a country)旅游。田中幸子对中国文化感兴趣，想多了解中国的少数民族文化，所以放假以后她打算和蒙古族(ménggǔ zú Mongolian)朋友一起回家，和中国人一起生活一段时间。

　　乔丹和别的同学不一样，他一直想当英语老师。这个假期他希望能找到一所中国的小学，教孩子们学英语。

　　还有一些同学，比如说山本一郎，因为特别不习惯早上8点上课，这个学期觉得特别累，很想每天睡懒觉(shuì lǎnjiào to get up late)，好好儿休息休息。

174

安娜听了同学们的假期计划，非常羡慕(xiànmù to admire)。原来她打算要么去旅游，要么继续学习汉语，可是爸爸妈妈非常想念她，希望她假期回国，所以放假以后她得回国。

2. 两人一组，和同伴一起回答下面的问题，并讨论一下课文是怎样介绍同学们放假以后的打算的。

Work in pairs and answer the following questions. Discuss how the text describes the plans for the vacation.

(1) 金大成放假以后有什么打算？为什么？

(2) 大卫和田中幸子有什么样的旅游计划？

(3) 乔丹为什么不出去旅游？

(4) 为什么山本一郎放假以后只想睡懒觉？

(5) 安娜这个假期做什么？原来她有什么计划？

● 给老师的提示：
这一题您可以带着全班一起完成，尽量启发学生注意课文每一段的主要内容。

3. 在班里调查一下，看看你们班的同学放假以后都打算做什么？

Take a survey of your class to find out what your classmates want to do during vacation.

姓　名	打算做什么	为　什　么

4. 利用下面的问题整理一下你调查的材料。

Use the following questions to organize your survey.

(1) 你们班有多少个同学，你调查了多少个同学？

(2) 你调查的同学中，大部分放假以后想干什么？他们的原因一样吗？

(3) 除了这些同学以外，别的同学想干什么？为什么？

(4) 你自己想干什么？为什么？

●给老师的提示：这一题主要是帮助学生确定写作内容和写作顺序的，所以，您可以引导学生有效地利用调查材料。

二、动手写 Getting It Down (约20分钟)

请你用20分钟写一段话，介绍一下你自己和同学们的假期计划。
Write a paragraph in 20 minutes, introducing you and your classmates' plans for vacation.

写后修改 After Writing (约10分钟)

1. 与同伴交换所写的短文，看后回答问题。
Exchange paragraphs with your partner, and then answer the questions.

(1) 他(她)写的句子你都能看懂吗？把看不懂的句子画出来，告诉他(她)。
Do you understand everything your partner wrote? Mark the unclear sentences and ask him/her.

(2) 比较一下你们俩写的这段话，看看你们介绍的同学们的假期计划一样不一样。
Compare your paragraph with your partner's and look at the differences in descriptions of the two plans.

(3) 你的同伴放假以后有什么打算，他(她)写清楚了吗？
What plans does your partner have for vacation? Does he/she write them clearly?

(4) 你的同伴有没有写错字？有的话就告诉他(她)。
Are there any wrong characters? If there are, tell him/her.

(5) 如果有你不知道的词和不认识的字，就问问他(她)。
If there are any characters you do not recognize, ask him/her.

(6) 有时间的话，帮同伴检查一下标点符号用对了没有。
If time permits, help your partner check the punctuation marks.

◈ 互相检查，改正错误，遇到困难可以问老师。
Check what your partner wrote and correct the errors. Ask your teacher when you encounter difficulties.

2. 改正自己短文中的错误，然后和其他小组交流一下。

Correct the errors in your paragraph and then discuss with other groups.

●给老师的提示：您可以请几个学生朗读他们的文章，使同学们分享彼此的写作成果。您还可以从学生的文章中总结一些实用的结构写在黑板上，最后做些简单、必要的讲解，作为本课的总结。

作业　Assignment

一、复习整理 Review

1. 整理本课所写过的句子和短文，把错句、错字改正后写在下边。

Review the sentences and paragraphs you wrote in this lesson, and correct the sentences and characters which were written incorrectly.

2. 整理本课所写过的句子和短文，将生词和新的结构找出来，写在下边，还可以用它们写几个新的句子，帮助自己记忆。

Review the sentences and paragraphs you wrote in this lesson. Pick out the new words and structures and write them down. Make some new sentences with them to help you memorize them.

二、补充提高 Growing and Improving

1. 对你写的短文再进行一次补充和修改，然后抄写在作业本上交给老师批改。

Revise the paragraph again and add the new content. Rewrite your paragraph and hand it in to your teacher.

2. 你的同学们在中国学完汉语以后都有什么打算？写一段话介绍一下。

What plans do your classmates have after they study Chinese in China? Write a paragraph about it.

◈ 要注意充分利用你在这一课学习的所有新词、新结构等，并尽量吸取其他同学文章中的成功之处。

Make use of the new words, structures, etc. in this lesson, and try your best to absorb the strong points from what your classmates wrote.

你抽烟吗

学习简单说明对某事的看法或态度

Learn to explain your opinions or attitudes about something

写前准备 Before Writing

一、热身活动 Warm-Up (约30分钟)

1. 仔细看看下面的图片，然后从小词库里选择词语写在合适的图片下边。
   Look at the following pictures, and then write the words from the Word Box under the appropriate pictures.

Word Box

> 困、累、喝酒、影响、咳嗽、烟、高兴、抽烟、阳台
> (yángtái balcony)、烟灰缸(yānhuī gāng ashtray)、聚会
> (jùhuì gathering)

_____

_____

_____

_____

香烟危害

Look at the following pictures, read, then write words from the list under the appropriate pictures.

2. 两人一组，看看你和同伴写的词语一样不一样，然后一起说说图片的内容。

Work in pairs. Look at whether the words you wrote under the pictures are the same as your partner's. Then discuss the pictures.

☀ 同伴说的时候，你应该注意听。如果有不知道的词语，一定要问问他(她)。

Listen to your partner carefully and ask him/her about the words that you don't understand.

3. 请在图片旁边为每一幅图片写几句话，简单介绍一下图片上的情况。

Write several sentences next to each picture, introducing it.

● 给老师的提示：这一题您可以采取先写后说的方式进行。

☀ 不会写的字，可以先用拼音写。

If there are any characters that you cannot write, you may write them in Pinyin first.

4. 两人一组，和同伴讨论一下为什么有很多人抽烟、为什么有很多人反对抽烟。将你们的看法简单填写在表格中。

Work in pairs discussing why many people smoke and why many people are against smoking. Fill in the table with your opinions.

人们抽烟的主要原因	人们反对抽烟的主要原因
(1)	(1)
(2)	(2)

☀ 只写出重要的词语或短语就可以了，不用写太多。

Just write key words or phrases. You don't need to write too much.

二、语言形式 Language Focus （约20分钟）

1. 和同伴一起看看下面的例句，并试着说几个新句子。
   Work with your partner to review the following example sentences, and then each says several sentences with each structure.

   - "连……也/都……"表示强调。例如：
     "连……也/都……" indicates emphasis. E. g.

     这个字连小孩子都认识。
     他连早饭也不吃，一起床就开始抽烟。
     他只坐了5分钟就走了，连他住哪儿我也忘了问。

   - "从……起"与表示时间、地点的名词性词语搭配，表示某一事情的开始时间和位置。例如：
     "从……起" is used with noun phrases like time or location phrases, indicating the starting time or location of something. E. g.

     她从三岁起，就喜欢唱歌跳舞。
     从现在起，我再也不抽烟了。

   - "一方面……一方面……"用于从两个角度说明一个问题的时候。例如：
     "一方面……一方面……" is used to explain an issue from two different angles.

     我不喜欢去卡拉OK，一方面是因为我不会唱歌，一方面是因为我不喜欢那么热闹。
     这样的活动一方面可以帮助大家提高汉语水平，一方面也可以使大家认识很多中国朋友。

2. 请你利用183页热身活动第4题表格中的内容写两段话，试着用一用"连……也/都……"、"从……起，……"或"一方面……一方面……"。
   Use the content in the No. 4 of the Warm-Up section on page 183 to write 2 paragraphs with "连……也/都……"，"从……起，……" or "一方面……一方面……".

(1) 人们抽烟的主要原因是什么？

_____

(2) 人们反对抽烟的主要原因是什么？

_____

●给老师的提示：这两题您可以采取先写后说的方式进行，并指导学生表达得更准确，更有条理。

写作任务　Writing Task

一、组织材料　Organizing Materials （约20分钟）

1. 阅读课文，并回答问题。
Read the text and answer the questions.

关于抽烟

　　大部分抽烟的人都认为抽烟有很多好处，比如累的时候抽一支烟，可以让自己更有精神；不抽烟不像男人等等。还有的年轻人觉得抽烟很时髦(shímáo fashionable)，拿着烟的样子很帅(shuài cool)，现在连一些女孩子也开始抽烟了。但是我认为，不管男女老少都不应该抽烟。

　　大家都知道，抽烟对自己的身体健康没有任何好处，抽烟的人更容易得癌症。抽烟还会影响别人的健康。如果在家里抽烟，会影响家人的身体健康；如果在公共场所(gōnggōng chǎngsuǒ public places)抽烟，那样就会影响大家的身体健康。另外，经常抽烟的人常常不停地咳嗽，不但自己不舒服，所有听到的人也感到很不舒服。还有，每年因为抽烟引起(yǐnqǐ to cause）的火灾(huǒzāi fire)也不少。

　　因此，为了自己和别人的健康，我认为大家都不应该抽烟。

2. 两人一组，和同伴一起回答下面的问题，并讨论一下课文是怎样表达自己的看法的。

Work in pairs to answer the following questions. Discuss how the text expresses its opinions.

(1) 抽烟的人认为抽烟有什么好处？

(2) 作者为什么认为大家都不应该抽烟？

(3) 作者的看法是什么？

●给老师的提示：这一题您可以带着全班一起完成，尽量启发学生注意课文是如何表达观点的。

3. 在班里调查一下，看看你们班有几个同学抽烟，他们对抽烟有什么看法。

Take a survey to see how many people in your class smoke and what opinions they have on smoking.

姓　名	是否抽烟	他(她)的看法

4. 利用下面的问题整理一下你调查的材料。
   Use the following questions to organize your survey.

   (1) 你们班有多少个同学，你调查了多少个同学？

   (2) 抽烟的多还是不抽烟的多？

   (3) 你觉得抽烟的同学们会不会戒烟(jiè xān to quit smoking)？ 为什么？

   (4) 你自己抽烟吗？ 为什么？

   ●给老师的提示：这一题是帮助学生确定写作内容和写作顺序的，所以，您可以引导学生抓住重点和特点从调查的材料中选择有用的来写。

二、 动手写 Getting It Down (约20分钟)

请你用20分钟写一段话，谈谈你对抽烟的看法。
Write a paragraph in 20 minutes expressing your opinions about smoking.

写后修改 After Writing (约10分钟)

1. 与同伴交换所写的短文，看后回答问题。
   Exchange paragraphs with your partner, and then answer the questions.

   (1) 他(她)写的句子你都能看懂吗？把看不懂的句子画出来，告诉他(她)。
       Do you understand everything your partner wrote? Mark the unclear sentences and ask him/her.

   (2) 他(她)对抽烟的看法都写清楚了吗？
       Does he/she make his/her opinions on smoking clear?

   (3) 比较一下你们俩写的这段话，看看你们对抽烟的看法一样不一样。
       Compare your paragraph with your partner's and look at whether you have the same opinions on smoking as your partner.

   (4) 你的同伴有没有写错字？有的话就告诉他(她)。
       Are there any wrong characters? If there are, tell him/her.

   (5) 如果有你不知道的词和不认识的字，就问问他(她)。
       If there are any characters that you do not recognize, ask him/her.

   (6) 有时间的话，帮同伴检查一下标点符号用对了没有。
       If time permits, help your partner check the punctuation marks.

   ❋ 互相检查，改正错误，遇到困难可以问老师。
   Check what your partner wrote and correct the errors. Ask your teacher when you encounter difficulties.

2. 改正自己短文中的错误，然后和其他小组交流一下。
Correct the errors in your paragraph and then discuss with other groups.

●给老师的提示：您可以请几个学生朗读他们的文章，使同学们分享彼此的写作成果。您还可以从学生的文章中总结一些实用的结构写在黑板上，最后做些简单、必要的讲解，作为本课的总结。

作 业　Assignment

一、 复习整理　Review

1. 整理本课所写过的句子和短文，把错句、错字改正后写在下边。
Review the sentences and paragraphs wrote in this lesson, and correct the sentences and characters which were written incorrectly.

2. 整理本课所写过的句子和短文，将生词和新的结构找出来，写在下边，还可以用它们写几个新的句子，帮助自己记忆。
Review the sentences and paragraphs you wrote in this lesson. Pick out the new words and structures and write them down. Make some new sentences with them to help you memorize them.

二、补充提高 Growing and Improving

1. 对你写的短文再进行一次补充和修改，然后抄写在作业本上交给老师批改。
Revise the paragraph again and add the new content. Rewrite your paragraph and hand it in to your teacher.

2. 写一篇短文谈谈你对喝酒的看法。
Write a paragraph to express your views on drinking alcohol.

❋ 要注意充分利用这一课所学的新词、新结构等，并尽量吸取其他同学文章中的成功之处。
Make use of the new words, structures, etc. in this lesson, and try your best to absorb the strong points from what your classmates wrote.

复习（三）

一、单元自测 Self-Test

按自测问题选择或填写。
Choose or fill in the form according to the self-test questions.

自测问题 Self-Test Questions	试着选择或写出你的答案 Choose or Write the Answers
1. 你现在能够简单、清楚地介绍你住的公寓或社区了吗？ Can you briefly and clearly describe your apartment or community?	A 能　B 还可以　C 不能
2. 请试着写出一些可以评价公寓、社区和服务项目的词语。 Try to write some words evaluating an apartment, community and its service facilities.	很好
3. 你知道怎样简单介绍一个地方了吗？ Do you know how to briefly introduce a place?	A 能　B 还可以　C 不能
4. 应该从哪几个方面介绍一个地方？请试着写出来。 From which aspects will you introduce a place? Write them down.	□　　　□ □　　　□
5. 你能简单介绍主要课程和学习情况了吗？ Can you briefly introduce your key courses and your studies?	A 能　B 还可以　C 不能
6. 介绍主要课程和情况时应该谈到什么内容？请试着写出来。 What will you introduce about your key courses? Write them down.	□　　　□ □　　　□

7. 你能简单、清楚地说明你的计划和打算了吗？ Can you briefly and clearly explain your plans?	A 能　B 还可以　C 不能
8. 请试着写出几个说明计划和打算时常用的词语。 Write some words about explaining plans.	想、要
9. 你能简单说明自己对一件事情的看法了吗？ Can you briefly explain your views on a matter?	A 能　B 还可以　C 不能
10. 请试着写几个在表达自己的看法时常用的词语？ Write some commonly-used words expressing your own views.	我觉得

二、复习与扩展　Review and Extension

1. 仔细看看图1，写出图中这个公园的特点。
   Look at the following picture 1 and write about the park's characteristics in the picture.

亭子 (tíngzi pavilion)

遇到生词可以查词典，也可以问问老师。

Ask your teacher or look up the new words in dictionary when you encounter them.

●给老师的提示：您可以让一两个组说一说他们所写的内容，以达到全班交流的目的。

2. 两人一组，讨论一下怎么利用自己写出的内容介绍这个公园。

   Work in pairs discussing how to use the content you wrote above to introduce this park.

3. 仔细看看图2，然后根据要求写句子。

   Look at the following picture 2 carefully and write sentences according to the requirements.

抱、盆(pén pot)、倒(dǎo to pour)、消防队(xiāofáng duì fire department)

已经发生的情况：

　　例：有一座房子着火了。

(1) _____

(2) _____

正在发生的情况：

例：一个人正在用灭火器 (mièhuǒqì fire extinguisher) 灭火 (mièhuǒ to put out a fire)。

(1) _____

(2) _____

将要发生的情况：

(1) _____

(2) _____

4. 全班讨论。说说你喜欢图2中的哪些人，不喜欢哪些人，理由是什么。
Whole-class discussion. Talk about people you like and dislike in the picture 2 and give your reasons.

5. 两人一组，和一个新同伴一起说说图2的内容。
Work in pairs. Talk about the picture 2 with a new partner.

●给老师的提示：您不妨找一两个组说一说，以达到全班交流、互相提示的目的。

三、写作工作室 Writing Workshop

有个中国朋友的孩子要去你们国家留学。他发来一封邮件向你了解情况。请给他回一封邮件。你的邮件中应该包括以下内容。

Suppose that a child of your Chinese friend intended to study in your country. He/She writes an email inquiring some information. Write a reply including the following content.

☐ 哪个学校比较好？为什么？

☐ 这所学校里边是什么样子？

□ 这所学校有哪些有趣的课程？

□ 为什么在这所学校上学？吃、住和学习方面很方便。

□ 你的其他想法和建议。

1. 按照下面的顺序整理一下关于上面几个方面的情况。
   Organize the materials according to the following order.

   1. 学校的名称：
      学校的优点：

   2. 学校的环境：

   3. 学校的课程种类：

   4. 学校内和周围有什么服务设施和服务项目：

   5. 你觉得来这个学校留学会有什么感觉：

   6. 你的建议：

   ☀ 这是准备，所以写出主要的词语或句子就可以了，不要写太多。不知道的情况可以问问你的同学们。
   This is a preparation activity, so just write key words or sentences. You don't need to write too much. Ask your classmates about what you don't know.

2. 请在20分钟的时间里，写出这个邮件的草稿。
   Write an email draft in 20 minutes.

◎ 你可以参考留言条的格式。
Refer to the format of a note.

3. 把草稿再检查修改一遍，重新抄写在一张纸上。如果你能在电脑上打出这些内容、发给老师最好。

Make a copy of the revised draft. It would be better to send it to your teacher by email.

4. 全班一起把大家写的收集起来，贴在大大的纸上，在教室里展示。

Collect the written emails of the entire class together and paste them onto a large piece of paper. Finally paste it onto the wall of your classroom.

词 汇 表

第一课

1. 按时 ānshí on time
2. 出差 chūchāi business travel
3. 饿 è hungry
4. 号码 hàomǎ number
5. 机场 jīchǎng airport
6. 留言 liúyán to leave a message
7. 麻烦 máfan troublesome
8. 手机 shǒujī cell phone
9. 条儿 tiáor note
10. 行李 xíngli luggage
11. 一直 yīzhí always
12. 原谅 yuánliàng forgive
13. 转告 zhuǎngào pass on

第二课

1. 不同点 bù tóng diǎn difference
2. 风景 fēngjǐng scenery
3. 个子 gèzi height
4. 国籍 guójí nationality
5. 基本 jīběn basic
6. 郊区 jiāoqū suburb
7. 经历 jīnglì experience
8. 辣 là spicy
9. 篮球 lánqiú basketball
10. 历史 lìshǐ history
11. 旅行 lǚxíng travel
12. 年龄 niánlíng age
13. 胖瘦 pàng shòu figure
14. 人口 rénkǒu population
15. 少数民族 shǎoshù mínzú minority group
16. 身高 shēngāo height
17. 瘦 shòu slim
18. 蔬菜 shūcài vegetable
19. 文化 wénhuà culture
20. 相同点 xiāngtóng diǎn similarity
21. 兴趣 xìngqù interest
22. 姓名 xìngmíng name
23. 性别 xìngbié sex, gender
24. 饮食 yǐnshí food and drink
25. 云南 Yúnnán Yunnan
26. 照片 zhàopiānr photograph
27. 专业 zhuānyè major
28. 足球 zúqiú football

第三课

1. 服装 fúzhuāng costume
2. 价钱 jiàqian price
3. 镜子 jìngzi mirror
4. 决定 juédìng decide
5. 砍价 kǎnjià bargain
6. 老板 lǎobǎn boss
7. 旗袍 qípáo cheongsam
8. 商场 shāngchǎng department store
9. 市场 shìchǎng market
10. 摊儿 tānr stall
11. 讨价还价 tǎo jià hái jià bargain
12. 颜色 yánsè color
13. 于是 yúshì then
14. 终于 zhōngyú at last

第四课

1. 厕所 cèsuǒ toilet
2. 房租 fáng zū rent (for a house, apartment, or building)
3. 干净 gānjìng clean
4. 公寓 gōngyù apartment
5. 合租 hé zū rent together with somebody else
6. 交 jiāo hand in
7. 交流 jiāoliú communicate
8. 介绍 jièshào introduce
9. 客厅 kètīng living room

10. 宽敞	kuānchang	spacious
11. 四合院	sìhéyuàn	compound with houses around a square courtyard
12. 套（量词）	tào	set(measure word)
13. 同屋	tóng wū	roommate
14. 卫生间	wèishēngjiān	bathroom, toilet
15. 卧室	wòshì	bedroom
16. 院子	yuànzi	courtyard
17. 钥匙	yàoshi	key
18. 脏	zāng	dirty
19. 中介公司	zhōngjiè gōngsī	agent
20. 租	zū	rent

第五课

1. 车票	chē piào	ticket
2. 窗	chuāng	window
3. 春	chūn	spring
4. 单衣	dān yī	unlined clothes
5. 地图	dìtú	map
6. 东	dōng	east
7. 短信	duǎnxìn	text message
8. 感觉	gǎnjué	feeling
9. 告别	gàobié	farewell
10. 候车室	hòuchē shì	waiting room
11. 火车站	huǒchē zhàn	railway station
12. 季节	jìjié	season
13. 绿	lù	green
14. 毛背心	máo bèixīn	a sleeveless woolen waistcoat
15. 毛衣	máoyī	sweater
16. 暖和	nuǎnhuo	warm
17. 晴	qíng	sunny
18. 秋	qiū	autumn, fall
19. 树叶	shùyè	leaf
20. 脱	tuō	take off
21. 外套	wàitào	coat
22. 夏	xià	summer
23. 香港	Xiānggǎng	Hong Kong
24. 阴	yīn	cloudy
25. 站台	zhàntái	railway platform

第六课

1. 打喷嚏	dǎ pēntì	sneeze
2. 肚子	dùzi	belly
3. 恶心	ě xīn	sick, feel like vomitting
4. 耳朵	ěrduo	ear
5. 发烧	fāshāo	fever
6. 后悔	hòuhuǐ	regret
7. 脚	jiǎo	foot
8. 酒	jiǔ	liquor
9. 拉肚子	lā dùzi	diarrhea
10. 凉鞋	liáng xié	sandals
11. 流鼻涕	liú bítì	runny nose
12. 难受	nánshòu	uncomfortable
13. 劝告	quàngào	advise
14. 嗓子	sǎngzi	throat
15. 书店	shū diàn	bookstore
16. 疼	téng	ache
17. 腿	tuǐ	leg
18. 胃	wèi	stomach
19. 温度	wēndù	temperature
20. 羊肉串	yángròu chuàn	lamb kebab
21. 腰	yāo	waist
22. 油腻	yóunì	greasy
23. 症状	zhèngzhuàng	symptom

第七课

1. 查	chá	look up
2. 臭	chòu	smelly
3. 词典	cídiǎn	dictionary
4. 打字	dǎ zì	type
5. 倒霉	dǎoméi	unlucky
6. 电灯	diàndēng	lamp
7. 电脑	diànnǎo	computer
8. 电梯	diàntī	elevator
9. 服务台	fúwù tái	reception desk
10. 服务员	fúwùyuán	receptionist
11. 害怕	hàipà	afraid
12. 坏	huài	bad
13. 空调	kōngtiáo	air-conditioner
14. 累	lèi	tired

15. 马桶	mǎtǒng	stool
16. 危险	wēixiǎn	dangerous
17. 洗衣机	xǐyījī	washing machine
18. 修	xiū	mend, repair
19. 转	zhuǎn	turn
20. 着急	zhāojí	worried

第八课

1. 帮	bāng	help
2. 车棚	chē péng	shed
3. 迟到	chí dào	late
4. 打听	dǎtīng	inquire
5. 端	duān	hold
6. 感谢	gǎnxiè	thank
7. 关心	guānxīn	care
8. 还	huán	give back
9. 急急忙忙	jí jí máng máng	hastily
10. 缴费单	jiǎo fèi dān	bill
11. 借	jiè	borrow, lend
12. 邻居	línjū	neighbor
13. 路人	lù rén	passerby
14. 迷路	mílù	lose one's way
15. 面条	miàntiáo	noodle
16. 求助	qiú zhù	ask for help
17. 热情	rèqíng	zeal
18. 热心	rèxīn	warm-hearted
19. 推	tuī	push
20. 修车铺	xiū chē pù	vehicle repairing stall
21. 嘱咐	zhǔfù	advise

第九课

1. 不知不觉	bù zhī bù jué	unconscious
2. 蛋糕	dàngāo	cake
3. 点（蜡烛）	diǎn (làzhú)	light (candles)
4. 寂寞	jìmò	lonely
5. 接受	jiēshòu	accept
6. 紧张	jǐnzhāng	nervous
7. 举行	jǔxíng	hold
8. 快乐	kuàilè	enjoyable
9. 蜡烛	làzhú	candle
10. 礼物	lǐwù	present, gift

11. 难忘	nánwàng	unforgettable
12. 日记	rìjì	diary
13. 伤心	shāngxīn	heartbroken
14. 生日	shēngri	birthday
15. 晚会	wǎnhuì	evening party
16. 无聊	wúliáo	boring
17. 响	xiǎng	aloud
18. 想念	xiǎngniàn	miss
19. 醒	xǐng	awake
20. 幸福	xìngfú	happy
21. 邀请	yāoqǐng	invite
22. 支（量词）	zhī (liàng cí)	branch (measure word)

第十课

1. 称	chēng	weigh
2. 秤	chèng	steelyard
3. 吃惊	chījīng	surprised
4. 结果	jiéguǒ	result
5. 经过	jīngguò	course
6. 渴	kě	thirsty
7. 路过	lùguò	pass by
8. 明白	míngbai	understand
9. 骗	piàn	deceive
10. 气	qì	angry
11. 生气	shēngqì	get angry
12. 随便	suíbiàn	casual
13. 忘记	wàngjì	forget
14. 西瓜	xīguā	watermelon

第十一课

1. 报纸	bàozhǐ	newspaper
2. 打扫	dǎsǎo	clean
3. 大厅	dàtīng	hall
4. 电子邮件	diànzǐ yóujiàn	email
5. 锻炼	duànliàn	exercise
6. 发（邮件）	fā (yóujiàn)	send (mail)
7. 饭馆	fànguǎn	restaurant
8. 附近	fùjìn	nearby
9. 公用	gōngyòng	public
10. 见面	jiànmiàn	meet
11. 健身房	jiànshēn fáng	gymnasium

12. 解决	jiějué	solve	
13. 咖啡馆	kāfēi guǎn	coffee shop	
14. 免费	miǎnfèi	free of charge	
15. 平时	píngshí	usually	
16. 日用品	rìyōngpǐn	daily commodities	
17. 上网	shàngwǎng	surf the Net	
18. 下棋	xià qí	play chess	
19. 小卖部	xiǎomàibù	small shop	
20. 小食品	xiǎo shípǐn	snack	
21. 阅览室	yuèlǎn shì	reading room	
22. 运动	yùndòng	sports	
23. 杂志	zázhì	magazine	
24. 座(量词)	zuò	used of large and solid things (measure word)	

第十二课

1. 北	běi	north
2. 操场	cāochǎng	playground
3. 长椅	chángyǐ	bench
4. 雕塑	diāosù	sculpture
5. 对面	duìmiàn	the opposite
6. 湖	hú	lake
7. 花	huā	flower
8. 教学楼	jiāoxué lóu	teaching building
9. 礼堂	lǐtáng	auditorium
10. 绿(草)地	lǜ (cǎo) dì	lawn
11. 门口	ménkǒu	doorway
12. 盆	pén	pot
13. 山	shān	hill, mountain
14. 树	shù	tree
15. 树林	shùlín	grove
16. 图书馆	túshūguǎn	library
17. 网球	wǎngqiú	tennis
18. 西	xī	west
19. 小路	xiǎo lù	lane

第十三课

1. 本子	běnzi	book
2. 笔记	bǐjì	note
3. 表达	biǎodá	express
4. 表演	biǎoyǎn	perform

5. 戴	dài	put on
6. 调查	diàochá	investigate
7. 耳机	ěrjī	earphone
8. 辅导	fǔdǎo	guide
9. 互相	hùxiāng	mutual
10. 教材	jiàocái	teaching materials
11. 课本	kèběn	textbook
12. 练习	liànxí	exercise
13. 任务	rènwu	task
14. 图片	túpiàn	picture
15. 完成	wánchéng	accomplish
16. 写作	xiězuò	writing
17. 学期	xuéqī	semester
18. 语法	yǔfǎ	grammar

第十四课

1. ……迷	mí	fan
2. 报名	bàomíng	sign up
3. 黑板	hēibǎn	blackboard
4. 计划	jìhuà	plan
5. 假期	jiàqī	vacation
6. 讲台	jiǎngtái	platform
7. 留	liú	leave
8. 蒙古包	měnggǔ bāo	yurt
9. 蒙古族	měnggǔ zú	Mongolian
10. 南方	nán fāng	south
11. 睡懒觉	shuìlǎnjiào	get up late
12. 美慕	xiànmù	admire

第十五课

1. 癌症	áizhèng	cancer
2. 比如	bǐrú	for example
3. 公共场所	gōnggòng chǎngsuǒ	public place
4. 好处	hǎochu	benefit
5. 喝酒	hē jiǔ	drink
6. 火灾	huǒ zāi	fire
7. 健康	jiànkāng	health
8. 戒烟	jiè yān	give up smoking
9. 精神	jīngshén	spirit
10. 聚会	jùhuì	gathering
11. 咳嗽	késou	cough

12. 空气	kōngqì	air		17. 烟	yān	smoke
13. 任何	rènhé	any		18. 烟灰缸	yānhuī gāng	ashtray
14. 时髦	shímáo	fashionable		19. 阳台	yángtái	balcony
15. 舒服	shūfu	comfortable		20. 引起	yǐnqǐ	cause
16. 帅	shuài	handsome				

汉语常用标点符号一览表

符号/名称	用法说明	例 句
，逗号	用于句子内部的一般停顿，单句里边的停顿，复句内分句之间的停顿。Used as a general pause in a sentence; separate in a simple sentence; separate the clauses in a complex sentence.	• 今天上午，我们参观了北京的胡同。 • 你起床以后先吃早饭，然后再去医院看病。 • 由于没有复习，考试时很多内容他都没有把握。
。句号	用于陈述句末尾的停顿。Used to mark the end of a declarative sentence.	• 北京是中华人民共和国的首都。
？问号	用于疑问句末尾的停顿。Used to mark the end of a interrogative sentence.	• 你想学什么专业？ • 难道你不相信我？
、顿号	用于句子内部并列词语之间的停顿。它表示的停顿比逗号短。Used to separate the parallel words. It indicates a shorter pause than commas.	• 我家院子里有桃树、苹果树和梨树。 • 我去过上海、杭州、西安等八个城市。
！叹号	用于感叹句或祈使句末尾的停顿，表示强烈的语气。Used to mark the end of an exclamatory or an imperative sentence. It indicates a strong emotion.	• 这里真是太美了！ • 赶快离开这儿！
；分号	用于复句内部并列小句之间的停顿。它表示的停顿比逗号长。Used to separate the paralleled simple sentences in a complex sentence. It indicates a longer pause than commas.	• 勤奋的人，为明天而努力；懒惰的人，只知道享受今天。

符号	说明	例子
： 冒号	用于提示性话语之后的停顿，用来提起下文。Used to pause after a reference term and introduce the following words.	• 他问我："你明天去哪里？" • 学院规定：旷课30节以上者，取消考试资格。
" " 引号	用来标明文章中直接引用的话或有特殊含义的词语。Used to enclose the direct speech or a term that is unusual.	• "外面有人找你。"她小声地对我说。 • "北大"是北京大学的简称。
…… 省略号	用来标明文章中省略了的话。Used to mark where sentences are omitted.	• 她哭着说："刚才它还在这儿，可是……" • 他目送着父亲走远，渐渐消失在黑夜中……
（ ） 括号	用来标明文章中解释性的话。Used to enclose the reference words.	• 土豆（学名马铃薯）是一种营养丰富的蔬菜。
《 》 书名号	用来标明书籍、报刊、文章、歌曲、戏剧等的名字或题目。Used to mark the name or title of the book, newspaper, essay, song and opera.	• 《三国演义》是中国古典名著。
—— 破折号	用来标明文章中解释说明的语句。Used to mark the reference terms in the context.	• 他这么努力，都是为了实现一个愿望——成为一名音乐家。
— 连接号	两个相关的名词构成一个意义时中间用连接号。相关的时间、地点或数目之间用连接号表示起止。Used to form a compound sense from two relative nouns. Used between dates, places or numbers to indicate the beginning and the ending.	• 放假时间为5月1日—5月8日。 • 北京—东京的航班就要起飞了。

重点提示

1. 逗号一定要写清楚,不能只点一个点儿(.),那样的话容易和顿号(、)混淆。

2. 两个句子的关系完全是并列的,中间就用分号(;);两个词语之间的关系完全是并列关系时,中间就用顿号(、)。

3. 括号和破折号不同,破折号引出的解释和说明,是正文的一部分,括号里的解释和说明不是正文,只是注释。

郑 重 声 明

高等教育出版社依法对本书享有专有出版权。任何未经许可的复制、销售行为均违反《中华人民共和国著作权法》,其行为人将承担相应的民事责任和行政责任,构成犯罪的,将被依法追究刑事责任。为了维护市场秩序,保护读者的合法权益,避免读者误用盗版书造成不良后果,我社将配合行政执法部门和司法机关对违法犯罪的单位和个人给予严厉打击。社会各界人士如发现上述侵权行为,希望及时举报,本社将奖励举报有功人员。

反盗版举报电话:(010)58581897/58581896/58581879

传　真:(010)82086060

E - mail:dd@hep.com.cn

通信地址:北京市西城区德外大街4号

　　　　　　高等教育出版社打击盗版办公室

邮　编:100011

购书请拨打电话:(010)58581118

图书在版编目（ＣＩＰ）数据

体验汉语写作教程. 初级. 2 / 陈作宏主编；陈作宏，
张璟，邓秀均编. —北京：高等教育出版社，2007.3（2008重印）
　ISBN 978-7-04-020675-3

　Ⅰ. 体… Ⅱ.①陈…②陈…③张…④邓… Ⅲ.汉语－写
作－对外汉语教学－教材 Ⅳ.H195.4

中国版本图书馆CIP数据核字（2007）第024486号

出版发行	高等教育出版社		购书热线	010 - 58581118
社　　址	北京市西城区德外大街4号		免费咨询	800 - 810 - 0598
邮政编码	100011		网　　址	http://www.hep.edu.cn
总　　机	010 - 58581000			http://www.hep.com.cn
			网上订购	http://www.landraco.com
经　　销	蓝色畅想图书发行有限公司			http://www.landraco.com.cn
印　　刷	涿州市星河印刷有限公司		畅想教育	http://www.widedu.com
开　　本	889×1194　1/16			
印　　张	13.75		版　　次	2007年3月第1版
字　　数	420 000		印　　次	2008年2月第2次印刷

本书如有印装等质量问题，请到所购图书销售部门调换。　　　　ISBN 978-7-04-020675-3

04900